TRAJECTORY

Living Into A Greater Story

Shannon Talor O'Brien

Forward By: Dr. Earl Lavender

ISBN (Paperback): 979-8-9889338-7-8
ISBN (eBook): 979-8-9889338-6-1

Table of Contents

Forward
By: Dr. Earl Lavender

I am so blessed! Understanding that my primary calling is to be a dedicated follower of Jesus Christ as Lord, my present assignment in that calling is to be a professor at Lipscomb University, which I have been at for over 30 years. Teaching at the graduate and undergraduate levels, my primary objective is to assist students and fellow scholars (as I regard my graduate students such as Shannon) in discovering and developing their gifts and talents in ways that bless others. When I see tangible goods to that end, I celebrate!

My undergraduate degree is in physical education, with a teaching and coaching emphasis. I am deeply grateful for that foundation. I have had the opportunity to play and coach various team sports, from youth athletics to professional baseball. At heart, I am a coach. A coach takes the athletes (or aspiring athletes) assigned to her or him, and works to help them develop their skills as individuals and as contributing elements of the team. I believe this coaching approach to life provides more opportunity to transform lives than preaching ever will. I wish more preachers/pastors/ministers were trained in coaching rather than oratory.

As you read and participate in this wonderful study, you will quickly understand why I absolutely love the work that coach Shannon Talor O'Brien has produced. You will find the format both compelling and extremely practical – a rare combination! Shannon, with the heart of a player-coach, shares her story as she invites you to consider your own. This work is rich in theological reflection, invitingly transparent in introspection, and transformative in application.

You will find this to be an incredibly helpful guide in what Paul challenges us to do in response to the Good News, "Don't copy the behavior and customs of this world, but let God transform you into a new person by changing the way you think. Then you will learn to know God's will for you, which is good and pleasing and perfect." (Romans 12:2 NLT) This is the journey coach Shannon invites you to pursue in this challenging, assessable, Spirit-filled work.

Do not cheat and go to the book's conclusion, but Shannon's advice for "where to go from here" is well worth the journey to get there! Imagine me grabbing my coaching whistle. Hear the shrill blast!

Envision me looking you in the eyes and saying, "You want to be a person for God's glory? Do you want to make a difference in this world, honoring its Creator? Then get ready for a rigorous workout – follow the plan. Like Paul, forget what lies behind and strain with every part of your body, mind, and soul, for the goal to be more like Jesus (Philippians 3:13, 14). It is one workout regimen that will exercise every part of your being. You will be changed!"

Thank you, Shannon. This is a wonderful sharing of your gifts as a dedicated disciple of Jesus, your excellent knowledge of God's word, and your loving concern for all (especially fellow athletes).

Introduction

I have worked in sports ministry for almost twenty years. I love it. In my experience, I have worked with many youth athletes to college athletes, professional athletes, Olympic & World Cup athletes. Here is what I have come to fully understand, we are all the same in our human condition regardless of our talent level achieved. We all want to do well, to be respected, to be known, and to feel like we matter. I believe this is part of our God given design; desiring to feel like we have something to offer and that it will make a positive impact for the greater good. This book is titled Trajectory because it is an invitation to consider where you are headed in life. All people are living their life on pathways to something. The question is, where are you headed?

Where do you desire to go? Do you desire to live into ways that lead to abundant living in Christ? What path leads to emptiness and isolation? While we can't control all of life's circumstances, we can choose the pathways that are towards becoming. All people are on a journey in life, and God thankfully meets us right where we are. He invites us to live out our personal life story in light of His story, which will affect the trajectory of where we are headed. The overarching narrative of God's story in Scripture is redemptive and illuminating; providing for us stories of others who have walked before us and encountered God in their journey. Each of their encounters were a trajectory game changer in their lives and what they pursued.

What follows in this devotional are a set of Training Days and Cool Downs designed to deepen your awareness of who you are and who God is. As an athlete and a coach, I understand and value the necessity to train, to study the game plan, and prepare for the battles that will come through sport. Athletes who are devoted to their sport make choices every day that revolve around having reverence towards their sporting demands.

1 Timothy 4:8-10 says, "For physical training is of some value, but godliness has value for all things, holding promise for both the present life and the life to come."

As Christ followers, we must also train our hearts and minds in Christ to pursue godliness. Godliness simply means to respond with reverence towards God in our life.

This devotional is structured to invite you into knowing the Lord more deeply as you discover more of your role in His story. The Training Ground and Cool Down sections will exercise your heart and mind to discover more about God and encourage you to reflect and stretch out your thoughts with Him. I encourage you to let God meet you right where you are. Be honest with yourself, and honest with Him, as you process the trajectory of your life and the story you are living into for your future.

Cheers to your journey! I pray this devotional is a great workout and strengthens your heart, mind, and soul as you pursue growing in knowing Him.

PART 1

Who Happens to Be

Through sports ministry I discovered that there is a significant difference between playing your sport and being a Christian, counter to being a Christian who plays a sport. Don't catch the difference? Let me explain.

When I was a Division 1 athlete at the at the University of Arizona it didn't take more than wearing your team's t-shirt to class to quickly be identified as a student athlete, and in that identification, it was typically a pretty regarded role. Additionally, I would wear a cross necklace, but that was under my soccer t-shirt, that was underneath my athletic identity. My first two years in college I identified myself as Shannon, a soccer player who happened to be a Christian. This was fine, more than fine, it was good. I wanted to be a Christian, but I loved my soccer identity more. Why wouldn't I? That is what the world around me most praised me for, most revered me for doing. Well, that was until we lost a game, or I had a bad spell in the goal. I was a goalkeeper, the hero or the loser. My worth ebbed and flowed depending on my performance and what others said about it. When I played well, lots of praise, pats on the back, "atta girl" comments, and I would feel great, I felt like I mattered, I felt like I was significant. But, on those off games, or average performances, I learned what a fair-weather fan was; I learned that through my identity in my sport, my performance equaled my worth.

I will never forget one of my first games during my sophomore year in college. I was the underclassman back up keeper, watching eagerly from the sideline when my coach called my name and told me to warm up. It was a warm night in the middle of the Arizona monsoon season, we had waited out a long lightning delay. About 70 minutes into the game my coach told me to warm up, we were already down 2-0 against our in-state rival. With 15 minutes left in the match, I'm subbed in. Wide eyed and nervous, the last thing I wanted to do was fail. Watching the play develop I prepared myself, a shot is taken, I see the ball flying towards me, right at me – no problem. I put my hands up, and before I could blink a second time, I hear cheers and groans, I see my teammates heads drop. The rain soaked ball slipped right through my hands and smacked the back of the net. Humiliating. My first few minutes in the match, and I gave up a goal that should have been an easy save. Embarrassed, I stand there in my eighteen-yard box adjusting my socks, feeling like a lone ranger with all eyes on me, any laughs or groans I hear I automatically assume it's at me. Stoically, I stand and look forward and watch my ten team-mates line up for another kick off. Thankfully those next ten minutes pass without any more epic fails. I jog off the field wanting to hide and avoiding eye contact, all while internally wishing someone would praise something I did well in those fifteen minutes to take the edge off my humiliation for my major blunder. Instead, my goalkeeper coach steps in front of me and tells me he is going to make me an eye appointment, "for there is no way you just missed it like that, surely your eyes are bad." Nodding my head, I comply and escape the field as quickly as I can. The next day, my coach picked me up in front of the McKale Center, our famed basketball team's arena, to drive me to the eye doctor. Getting in the car we exchange typical friendly hellos, but drive most of the way in awkward silence. I gaze out the car window as green flashes of saguaro cactus' zoom past the tan desert sand rooted under the vast blue sky. Along the way, I contemplated the game the night before, and how it could have gone if I had just made that catch. I am really hoping that my eyes are bad, because that would be just the perfect excuse for why I missed such an easy routine save. Eagerly I walk into the appointment ready to please. Twenty minutes later, to my chagrin, my vision is reported to be 20/20. Dang it. My coach looks at me and shakes his head. I feel ashamed. I feel like an idiot. The chatter in my head goes from bad to worse, beating myself up, agreeing with him that I should have done better, that I blew an opportunity, that I cost the team a goal and negatively affected my and our team's goals against average. Riding back, I don't remember all that we chatted about, I just knew that the next few weeks of training were going to be difficult; that I would be put through the gauntlet for both my blunder and the embarrassment my coach felt for my poor performance in those first five minutes of that game.

My identity at that point in my playing career was wrapped in my performance. My worth was only being defined by what I did or didn't do. In those weeks following, my goalkeeper coach bought a ball machine used for soccer, much like a pitching machine used for baseball. I will never forget standing there in the Arizona sun, desperately wanting to catch these fast flying knuckle ball "shots" that zipped in at me like Messi himself was striking the ball fifteen yards from my face. Let me just say that it didn't help my case. The season wrapped up, and I felt like a loser, a loser who happened to be a Christian.

You see, it wasn't until a couple years later while playing semi-professional soccer for a soccer team owned by Missionary Athletes International that I began to be trained in learning more about my identity. Through the course of the time that passed from that first blunder to finishing my senior year at Arizona as the then Pac-Ten leader in saves, I began to realize what God had been transforming in me. My worth and my significance could not be in my sport, it could not be in *anything* that I did. My worth and my significance instead needed to be in Whose I was, and in what God declared true over me. My identity shifted when I began to anchor my worth in Christ and to see myself as a Christian who happened to be a soccer player (instead of being a soccer player who happened to be a Christian). That first line of identity is our anchor, our "who." As I began to anchor myself in Christ and find my worth in Him, soccer was just something I did, not something that I was. I love how Christine Cain has coined this phrase, she says, "God separates our who from our do."[1] This is why God can extend forgiveness and grace for our sin, our shortcomings, and blunders. God sees us for who we are (His creation), not for what we do (in blunders or successes).

When we find our worth in Christ alone, based on what He did on the cross for us, and based on what He says is true about us; our feeling of significance does not have to wane like it does when we find our worth in our performance and what other people say about us. This was extremely freeing for me. Did I still want to play well? Of course I did. Did I hope others praised my performance? Absolutely! It is in our human nature to want to do well. It is in our human nature to desire being known and to contribute to this world, this is not sinful, in fact it is how God designed us. But understanding how our original created design is corrupted by our sinful nature is really important, and necessary in discerning how to live into God's created order and resting our significance in His story.

This is where trajectory comes in. Trajectory is simply a pathway in which an object or a person is headed towards. As a Christ following human, we will wrestle with the flesh of our humanness and the embodying power of the Holy Spirit working in our life. One of the first critical steps on our trajectory journey is discovering where our worth and significance can come from and how that then informs our being and our doing.

Day 1 | The Training Day: Identity & Significance

Grab a journal and something to write with as we begin to unpack a few questions throughout our "Training Day" times together. Today, we are going to look at where we find our significance and identity.

Identity is defined as a sense of who you are, how you are related to other people. Significance is defined as someone or something that is necessary to a cause or operation. Someone of consequence; noteworthy, meaningful, out of the ordinary, valuable or important.

- Where are some places in your life that you look to find significance and worth?
- What are some sources in our culture that communicate to us if we matter?

- Your worth does not have to be in what you do, or what others say; how much does social media affect your life? How much do the opinions of others affect how you feel about yourself?
- What if, instead your worth and significance was anchored in what God says is true about you?

See the list below, read the statements from Scripture declaring the truth about you in Christ. This list was shared with me years ago and it still offers me insight and perspective when my flesh is inclined to find my worth through other people's opinions and my performance. As you read the statements below, star the statements that are easy for you to believe. Circle the statements that are hard for you to believe. In Christ...

1. I am accepted and worthy.
   (Romans 15:7; Psalm 139)
2. I am never alone.
   (Hebrews 13:5b; Romans 8:38,39)
3. I am adequate.
   (2 Corinthians 3:5-6; Philippians 4:13)

4. I have boldness and confidence.
   (Proverbs 3:26; Hebrews 10:19)
5. God is faithful to me.
   (Philippians 1:6; 2:13;
   2 Thessalonians 3:3)
6. I have the mind of Christ.
   (1 Corinthians 2:16; 2 Timothy 1:7)
7. I have hope.
   (Psalm 62:5; Romans 15:13;
   Colossians 1:27)
8. I am seen as perfect.
   (Hebrews 10:14; Colossians 2:13)
9. I have been chosen and set apart.
   (Ephesians 1:4; 1 Peter 2:9)
10. I lack nothing. (Philippians 4:19)
11. I am free from fear.
    (Psalm 34:4; 2 Timothy 1:7)
12. I live by faith,
    (Romans 1:17; 2 Corinthians 5:7)
13. I have strength.
    (2 Samuel 22:33; Psalm 28:7)
14. I have victory.
    (Proverbs 2:7-8; Romans 8:37)

15. I have wisdom.
    (Proverbs 2:6-7; 1 Corinthians 1:30)
16. I am free.
    (2 Corinthians 3:17; Romans 6:18)
17. I have comfort. (2 Corinthians 1:3,4)
18. I am protected. (Psalm 18:2; 32:7)
19. I am perfectly loved.
    (Romans 8:38,39; Ephesians 2:4-5; 5:1-2)
20. I am an adopted child of God.
    (Romans 8:16; Galatians 4:6-7;
    Ephesians 1:5)
21. I am totally forgiven.
    (Psalm 103:12; Ephesians 1:7)
22. I have been declared righteous.
    (Romans 3:24; 1 Corinthians 1:30)
23. I am indwelt by the Holy Spirit.
    (Acts 1:8; Galatians 4:6; 1 Corinthians 3:16)
24. I have direct access to God.
    (Ephesians 2:6; Hebrews 4:16)
25. I am blameless. (Jude 1:24; Romans 8:1)
26. I have been created for good works.
    (Ephesians 2:10)
27. I am a new creation. (2 Corinthians 5:17)

28. I have authority over Satan.
    (1 Peter 5:8,9; I John 4:4)
29. I have peace with God. (Romans 5:1-2)
30. I am a light in the world. (Matthew 5:14)
31. I have an eternal inheritance.
    (Romans 8:16-17; Ephesians 1:14,18)
32. I have been raised with Christ.
    (Romans 6:4-8; Galatians 2:20)
33. I will be with Christ in heaven.
    (2 Corinthians 5:1; Philippians 3:20)
34. I have eternal security. (1 John 5:11-13)
35. I have spiritual gifts for His Kingdom.
    (1 Corinthians 12)

- Which of these thirty-five statements do you find hardest to believe?
- Which statements stood out to you the most? Why?
- As you begin to think about what God declares true about you, how does this identity awareness begin to shift your thinking about yourself?
- Take a moment to pray – Ask God for what you need. Tell God what you are

feeling and let yourself meet with Him in what you're processing.

Day 1, The Cool Down: Significance & Identity

Spend some time exhaling and stretching out your thoughts. Fill in the blanks according to you.

I am [insert name] _______________________
a Christian, who happens to be a [insert what you do/play, etc.] _______________________
__________.

(Example: I am Shannon O'Brien, a Christian, who happens to be a coach and a retired soccer player.)

When we anchor our identity in Christ, understanding who we are in what He declares true about us, we are freed from the bondage of living under the opinions of others.

- How does basing your personal identity in God's truth reframe your perspective that God cares more about who you are than what you do?

- Close in prayer. Name what you are feeling and desiring. Ask Jesus to help you find your worth in Him. I encourage you to write down the Truth statements that God declares true over you and place them where you will see them throughout your day. This is an active way to renew your mind and train your heart to both feel and know your worth in Christ.

Day 2 | The Training Ground: Likeness & Justification

We have been looking at finding our identity in who we are in Christ, and not in what we do. It's convicting to me when I realize how much power I can give someone else through their opinion of me. We are bombarded by social media and the influencing messages projected through a screen. Those messages are typically suggesting that there is more to improve on or to acquire. But, what if instead, we looked at how we ought to be through God's eyes, instead of the world's?

We are going to do some Bible aerobics today, read the following verses and write down what you learn about who you are:

Read Genesis 1:26-27; 2:7; 5:1-2 in the Old Testament and 1 Corinthians 11:12 from the New testament:

- Whose likeness/image is humankind made in? Who breathed life into us?
- Where do both man and woman come from?

Read Ephesians 4:24

Humans were created according to God's likeness in righteousness and holiness.

The word righteousness in Greek is *dikaio-syne*, which means in a broad sense "state of him who is as he ought to be; the condition acceptable to God; which includes correctness of thinking, feeling, and acting."[2] This same word is used in Romans 3:21-22 and verse 23 for the word justified. The word holiness in Greek is *hosiotes*,[3] which means to have devotion towards God; being faithful in fulfilling the duty of being devoted to God.

Read Romans 3:21-26

- Where does righteousness come from, and what does it come through?
- What have all done?
- How is one justified?

When we invite and receive God's life into our personal life, we are not justified by anything that we do, but by what Christ has done through His death and resurrection. We are justified only by what Jesus has done. God provides righteousness (justification) to us through our faith in Christ. This is significant to understanding our identity in Christ. We can rest in our identity in Christ, solely based on what Jesus did in dying on the cross, paying the penalty for our sinful condition, and reconciling us back to God through His resurrected life. Our salvation is secure in what Jesus did for us. When we put our faith (trust) in Christ for our salvation, we are provided a

God-given capacity to grow and mature into the likeness of Christ. Our salvation is secure in who Jesus is, and His obedience through the Cross. Jesus knew His purpose in life was to actively participate in the mission of His Heavenly Father, which is to reconcile humankind from their sinful condition and restore humankind as they ought to have been: set apart and approved by God.

Read Colossians 3:10,12

- Whose image are we being renewed in?

Read Ephesians 6:14 and Isaiah 59:17

- What are we to put on in Ephesians in verse 14?
- What did God put on in Isaiah 59:17?

Zeal in Hebrew is *qin'ah*[4], which means jealousy, ardor, which is a disposition of being jealous *for* a person you love, having a passion *for* them. In Isaiah 59:17 the context of this scripture is saying that God wrapped himself in jealous love *for* His creation. In personal application, it means he wrapped himself in jealous love *for* you.

Read Isaiah 9:7 and 37:32

God covered his chest with the body armor of righteousness (Justice), He covered his mind with the confidence of deliverance, He clothed Himself to avenge our fallen condition. It was His love, His passionate jealousy (zeal) *for you,* to be reconciled back to Him that accomplished this.

There is a significant difference between being jealous *for* someone and their attention, compared to being jealous *of* someone. My husband is a head coach at the division one level, he is busy. He is on the road recruiting half the time when he is not in season with the team playing both home and away games. My husband, and our two children are used to this schedule, it is the demand of our vocational ministry. However, it is not inappropriate for me or our kids to be jealous *for* his attention when he is home. Sometimes the timing of his recruiting calls are in the evening, we can overhear him on the phone being intentional in asking questions and seeking to know the player he is recruiting. Playfully one day, I said to him, "recruit me." In the essence of that statement I was communicating, "I want your undivided attention too, I want you to also seek to know me." He chuckled with me, but it was a message we both needed to be reminded of to attune our intentionality with one another in our marriage and family. It is completely appropriate for our kids to have zeal for their daddy, and for him to have zeal for their attention. Now when my husband comes home from a trip and the kids or I are preoccupied with something we are doing, he will jokingly say to us, "recruit me." This is what being jealous *for* looks like, it is a healthy and appropriate passion that drives us to pursue relationship. God is jealous *for* you, he is recruiting you, and He appropriately desires for you to give Him your attention and pursue relationship with Him.

Day 2, The Cool Down: Likeness & Justification

Spend a few moments journaling, exhale and stretch out your thoughts on paper.

- Is there a personal relationship in your life that you have longed for? A person you have been jealous *for* their attention, their time?
- Why is it appropriate for you to desire this?
- How does relating to what you feel for that earthly relationship help you understand what God's desire is in connecting with you in a personal relationship with Him?

After reflecting on the above questions, close in prayer. Exhale your desires and longings to the Lord. Inhale His love and zeal for you.

Day 3 | The Training Ground: Chosen Representative

We have been looking at how our identity in Christ is transformational in how we find our worth and significance. In the last section, we looked at what zeal means, and how it is appropriate to be jealous for a relationship with a loved one, and that God's zeal for us is what motivated

Him to reconcile us back to Him. Today we are going to look at what it means to be a chosen representative of God.

Read 2 Corinthians 5:16-21

- Anyone in Christ is a what?
- What is the ministry God is giving us? What message has he committed to us?
- We are to be Christ's what? In verse 20, what are we called to be? Why?

God is working in and through his creation to effect change, providing saving restorative justice. The mission of God is universal, and God's people are to be His ambassadors, allowing God to make His appeal through us for others. As an ambassador, that means we are a chosen representative of the King. More specifically, as Christ's ambassadors we are to go, to speak, and honor Jesus as a representative of Him in all that we do. The people of God are to be countercultural, and a distinctive people displaying an attractive lifestyle to God's glory before surrounding nations.

We are to be a "so that" people like Jesus was/is for us. God desires to make his appeal through us for the sake of others to also want to get in on what God has done, is doing, and will do. We are to be an Ambassador of Christ so that other people might know God's salvation and receive restorative justice.

Read 2 Corinthians 5:20-21

- What are we to become?
- Who provided the way *so that* we could become this?

Here is that word again, as we looked at on Day 2, righteousness, in Greek is *dikaiosyne*, which means we are to be as we ought to have been in God's original creation. That is, in Christ reconciling us, we become the condition acceptable to God; which includes the capacity to grow in correctness of thinking, feeling, and acting. We have God's favor when we are in Christ; we are Divinely approved. How about that for an identity check? Everything in this world we live in creates a tension in "measuring up." In Christ, we are approved by God, and chosen to represent Him, what an incredible honor and privilege.

I will never forget the first time I was invited to put on a professional soccer jersey that not only had my last name on the back with a number, but more excitingly, was the name of the team on my chest that I was representing. I was identified as part of that team, chosen and identified as one of them. In Ephesians 6:14, when we read the command for us as Christ followers to put on the breastplate of righteousness, it is like an athlete putting on their team's jersey. We are identifying whose team we are on, and we are battling as representatives of that team's ownership and all who are associated with that team.

God has chosen you. He has chosen you to represent His team. You have been justified through Jesus Christ's work on the Cross in His death and resurrection. Once you put your trust in Christ and join His team, there is nothing you can or can't do that will disqualify you from His team. With that, as an ambassador of Christ, we also have the great privilege to be responsible in how we live to best represent Jesus and His story. God has created us with free will, which is affected by our sinful condition. It is our choice to put on that Divinely approved breastplate and operate from a mindset and diligence of Christ to combat a very real enemy (Satan) that wants to rob, kill, and destroy us. Additionally, we need to consciously clothe ourselves in Christ to combat our flesh, our natural sinful state of our human condition. By consciously putting on our breastplate of righteousness, we are choosing to guard our hearts and claim our identity in Christ. Doing this daily helps us armor up to be a *so that* people. This is significant to our identity. This is also significant in helping us live out our story in the trajectory of God's story and representing Him well.

Day 3, The Cool Down: Chosen Representative

Spend a few moments journaling, exhale and stretch out your thoughts on paper.

- How does knowing you are chosen by God encourage you? How do you feel, knowing He approves you, solely based

on what Christ has done, and not on anything that you could or couldn't do?
- What intimidates you about being an Ambassador for Christ, a representative of Him?
- As a Christian who happens to be ___________________ (fill in the blank as it pertains to you), how are you going to be an ambassador for Jesus amongst the people you do life with?

Close in prayer. Tell God what you're learning, seeing or noticing, and feeling. Ask God to help you represent Him well. Ask Him to help you rest in His truth and faithfulness.

PART 2

Understanding our Fallen Condition

It was another peaceful day in the Garden full of harmony and wholeness. Adam and Eve were living in oneness with God, their created design, until a crafty serpent entered the scene and imposed doubt in the mind of Eve. The serpent questioned God, and suggested deception in the life Adam and Eve were living. Satan asked, "Did God really say…?" baiting Eve to wonder and doubt the goodness of God and her created role. From there, Adam and Eve engaged in doubting God, and separation occurred as a byproduct of freewill operating in self-reliance instead of God-reliance. When Adam and Eve ate the fruit, all of creation was thrown into chaos and fell from harmony. The Fall's terms and conditions involve separation from God due to sin which includes the conditions of selfishness, brokenness, disorder, pain, suffering, and death. Humankind was exiled from the Garden of Eden where it's created design was intended to live into wholeness and abundance with God. In this exile, while God is Holy (set apart) He still desired oneness with His creation. So ever since the Fall, He has been pursuing His creation, seeking to redeem and restore it to its intended design.

We see throughout the biblical story God providing human figures to lead Israel out of bondage. With Moses, God leads the Israelites on an Exodus journey towards the Promise Land, but the sinful nature of humans causes them to fall short; they are not fully faithful to the mission. Hundreds of years pass, and then God breaks into the world through a baby named Jesus, Emmanuel, God with us. Jesus recapitulates atonement, and in His faithful first order story (the personal narrative of his life), He lives into God's redemptive narrative, and fulfills

God's redeeming mission by being obedient to death on the cross; which is the paradigm that affords all of creation, life and redemption through His resurrection.

On a historical timeline, we live on this side of the cross, but we are still in the "not yet" of New Creation being fully restored. Like Adam and Eve, our default human nature is still inclined to doubt God and make self-reliant choices that cause us to live into the Fallen broken world's story. However, in Christ, we have been invited into a Greater Story, one that holds promises of faithfulness, and offers us purpose within our own personal first order story. God's Greater Story beckons us to live on mission presently and become a *so that* people that serves as a signpost to the New Creation to come. The question is, if we choose to live into God's redemptive second order story as Christ followers, then how do we effectively live out our personal first order story affected by the Fall and our sinful condition?

I believe there is power in an invitation. To be asked to get in on something, invited to experience something with others is special.

As an athlete, being invited to be part of the team, to train in community and participate in a united goal is both a privilege and a responsibility. Spiritually, our life has been given two different team invitations to consider joining: we can either choose to accept God's invitation and join His team, or by default, remain on the Fallen world's team. To explain this concept more theologically, we live in a fallen world that offers two competing stories to frame our life with. Stories involve a sequence of events that share a narrative of a person's journey. Our personal life story is known as our "first order story," and in that we will seek to make sense of our life. The notion of meaning making is part of our human wiring. All of us are offered two secondary meta-narratives that are competing stories, we will either frame our personal first order story with the meta-narrative that our fallen world and culture offers us, or we can frame our personal narrative with God's Story, a redemptive alternative second order story that will affect our eternal trajectory.

By default, in our humanity we will frame our first order story in a second order story in an effort to make meaning of life. The world has offered us the idea of "YOLO" and a "cancel culture," living out life in the mission of "me" and canceling out others by shaming and rejecting them. This is the opposite of how God has treated us. The world tells us daily that it is hurting, that it is corrupt, that it is full of chaos. Social media offers us a distorted perception of the "good life" and leads us to chase after contentment through the means of consumerism and status; which is incessant. I will never forget the morning after I played for a National championship, I awoke, looked at the clock and thought to myself; "well now what?" I realized that training would need to start again because there was another title to chase. This is the essence of the world, it never fully satisfies. This is the default second order story the world offers us, but we don't have to frame our life with that narrative, we have been invited into a Greater Story. God's redeeming second order story is unique and Jesus offers us a startlingly different way of pursuing life. Jesus' atonment offers us the Kingdom of God, and invites us to live out our unique personal story framed in His alternative second order story that provides hope, redemption, and opportunity to represent Him and impact the broken world by partnering with Christ in His redemptive mission in the world. Instead of abandoning us, God recruits us and invites us to do life with Him on His team.

Day 4 | The Training Ground: Conflicting Kingdoms

Depending on which second-order story you are framing your life with will affect the trajectory of your everyday living. As we read on Day 3 in part one, Christ has invited us to be His Ambassador, to represent Him in our personal life stories. God has created us with a purpose that is for His glory, which is to be rooted in our identity in Christ, and live into His story of reconciliation *so that* the righteousness of God can be experienced amidst the culture we live in.

Read 1 John 2:15-17

The word "world" here is not the world of people or the created world, but is referring to realm (kingdom) of sin which is influenced by Satan and organized against God's righteousness. For example, in verse 15 you could read it as, "Do not love the kingdom of sin or anything in the kingdom of sin."

Read 1 John 5:17, 21 and Colossians 3:5-10

- What belongs to our earthly nature? Which is what? (See Colossians 3:5)

The Greek word for idolatry is *eidolatria* in Colossians 3:5, which means to "worship or service of an image."[5]

- What are we to keep ourselves from? (see 1 John 5:21)

Idols are anything that keeps us or takes us from the heart of God. Worship means to show adoration or reverence. We are designed to worship God, but there are many things in the kingdom of sin that tempt us to worship them instead of God. This is the condition of our Fallen human nature.

Read Galatians 5:16-21

- What are we to live by?
- In living by the Spirit, what will we not gratify?
- Our sinful nature is in conflict with what?
- In verse 21, what will we not inherit if we live into the realm of sin?

Read Romans 14:17-18

- What are the characteristics of the Kingdom of God?
- Who are we serving when we live this way, and who is it pleasing to?

Read Galatians 5:22-26

- What has been crucified if we belong to Christ Jesus?
- What are we to live by, and who are we to keep in step with?
- What are we not to become?
- What are the fruits of the spirit?

Day 4, The Cool Down: Conflicting Kingdoms

Spend a few moments journaling, exhale and stretch out your thoughts on paper.

- What are things in the 'kingdom of sin' that tempt you to find your worth in them, and worship them in the place of God?
- Does social media primarily encourage you or discourage you?
- What kinds of images do you post on social media? What's your motive for doing so?
- Is there anything unhealthy or idolatrous (image-worship) in your social media use? In your everyday way of living?
- When you live by your sinful nature, who are you serving?
- Which kingdom (God's or sin) is most influencing how you live your life? When you live by the Spirit, who are you serving?

Jesus cares about the direction of your life, not the perfection of it. Christian living isn't supposed to be about legalistic do's and don'ts. It's instead to be about the condition of our heart, our wellspring, and surrendering our self reliance to become Christ reliant. How we choose to live is a reflection of the kingdom we are serving. We were designed to live in righteousness and wholeness through Christ. In Christ, it is His Spirit that is at work helping us to do as we ought to do, for God's glory and our blessing.

- How does this make you feel? What is being stirred in you? What is God inviting you into with Him in your personal life at this time?

Close in prayer. Tell God what you are feeling and thinking. Ask Him to help you live into His Kingdom for His glory.

Day 5 | The Training Ground: Our Condition

As we looked at yesterday, there are two kingdoms that are in conflict with one another, and both are going to tug at our heart. The world offers us vast options that are incessant to chasing satisfaction. The world's story is about the individual, about chasing fame, fortune, and influence; pursuing life to satisfy our selfish nature, which is an aspect of our fallen human condition. The word "sin" is used in the sport of archery. When an archer is aiming to hit the center spot on the bullseye, if they miss the center mark, then it is called a sin. No matter how close or how far off they are from that perfect center, it's a sin. Sin in the story of God is not wrong doing, it is wrong being. Because we are born of a sinful Fallen world, our human condition misses the mark from the beginning. We need God, we need to be born again through Christ to transform our condition. Our human condition affected by the Fall is inclined to operate in deliberate and empathic independence of God. When Adam and Eve chose to entertain the doubt that Satan created in the Garden and they acted on eating the fruit, eternal separation was the result. In their self-reliance, they broke their fellowship with God.

Fellowship is walking closely with God in a personal relationship with Him. We are born with a sinful condition due to the Fall, but we can have new life through Christ renewing us daily. A relationship with God is secure through the work Jesus did on the cross, not by anything that we can do. Christ's death and life resurrected, provided us a way back to how we "ought to have been," which is in relationship and fellowship with God. Through the Holy Spirit, the life of Christ can permeate our heart (wellspring), and transform our sinful nature so that we are able to live into the trajectory of Christ's righteousness.

Living into righteousness takes the reconciliation of Christ working in our lives, and transforming our sinfulness. We are given free will to live as we want to, and with that, the desire of the Lord is that we would want to walk closely with Him. Because God is Holy, He cannot participate in sin with us, but He can restore us from our sin through our willingness to confess and repent of our sinful ways. We are secure in our relationship with God, because of the covenant He manages, and He is faithful to His commitment to us. The challenge is, we are unfaithful towards God due to our sinful nature. When we sin, we break fellowship with God. Tangibly, we also see this reality of relationship and fellowship in our human relationships and friendships. When two people are in a relationship or friendship, they will have fellowship when things are going well, but when there is sinful behavior that causes them to feel a disconnect, their fellowship is broken. Two people can still be in a relationship but they may not be talking to one another or willing to be around one another because they are at odds with one another. Same is true with God and us. Sin breaks fellowship with God and with other people in our lives. The good news is, God is always willing to reconcile and will receive our confession. The reality however, is that our sinful human nature can be stubborn and withhold reconciliation from people and God. To restore fellowship, we need to practice confession. James 5:16 says, "Therefore confess your sins to each other and pray for each other so that you may be healed. The prayer of a righteous person is powerful and effective." To confess means to admit whole-heartedly without reservations, to openly declare and acknowledge the wrong you have committed. When we confess our sin, and acknowledge it before God and before the people who we have wronged, reconciliation can begin to happen and fellowship can begin to be restored with forgiveness.

Read Colossians 2:6

- Who are we to continue to journey with and allow to shape our lives?

Read Psalm 32:5-6 and 1 John 1:9

- What are we to acknowledge? What are we to confess?
- What did God do with our sin?

When we fully confess our sin to God, we are forgiven for it; and this restores fellowship in our secure relationship with God.

Read 1 John 5:19-21

- What are we called in verse nineteen?
- What is under the control of evil one?

This is really important to understanding our identity in Christ, as well as understanding whose "jersey" we are wearing and the opponent we are up against. We are called the children of God. The Greek word for 'world' in this verse is cosmos, and means "ordered system," including the universe, the worldly affairs, and inhabitants of the world who are alienated from God.[6] This is significant. The ordered system of the world is vulnerable to the influence of the evil one, Satan. When we ask, "Why do bad things happen?" It's because of the Fall and how the sinful nature of humankind is affected by evil and the degeneracy of creation from how it ought to have been from Genesis. While God is soverign, it's important to recognize that the world, the entire created order of the cosmos and everything in it has been affected by the Fall due to sin. Our fallen human condition is subject to sin, wrong being, which leads to wrong doing. When we accept Christ's atonement for our sin and receive Him as our Savior, we are no longer servants to sin, we have been reconciled through Christ. In this reconciliation, we still can be affected by our sinful nature, and need to be intentional in allowing Christ's nature to shape us and transform sinfulness.

Read Romans 6:15-18

The word slave here probably made you squirm, it did for me. In the Greek, this word is *doulos*[7], meaning servant, or devoted to another to the disregard of ones' own interests. It is important to recognize, spiritually speaking, we are either servants to sin, or servants to righteousness. After what we learned about our identity the past few days, I don't know about you, but I would rather rest in the peace of being Divinely approved and be a devoted servant to Christ and His mission to reconcile the world to God. We are justified by the work Jesus did, and not on anything that we can do. In Christ, it is a privilege and a blessing to be devoted to Christ's interests and allow His story to influence my way of living. Otherwise, we are servants to wrong being and stuck in bondage to our fallen condition that keeps us on trajectory to further isolation and brokenness.

Satan is crafty, and he has so cleverly manipulated the general public to believe that God is unjust and unloving; when in actuality, it is Satan who is the ruler of evil, and he is the one who is unjust and unloving. When bad things happen in this world, Satan is behind it, and our own sinful nature leads us astray.

Read James 1:13-18

- In verse 14, what are we tempted by?

When I read this verse, it really struck me. It is informing me to realize that I am tempted by my own evil desires. Now, I would have never identified myself as "evil." For that is a word that suggests death and unjust cruelty. But if I take this verse to heart, I need to realize that my sinful nature is malignant. I need help to overcome my unhealthy, inwardly foul sinful nature.

When I was a freshman in high school, my mom was diagnosed with stage 4 breast cancer; she had 19 out of 20 lymph nodes infected and 4 spots on her liver. She had a mastectomy on her right breast where once the tumor was removed, an open cavity was left on her chest, there was not enough flesh available to close up the wound. Every morning, my 5-year-old brother sat by my father as he packed the wound with fresh gauze. My mom went through heavy chemo and was put on a macrobiotic diet. She went from a size 12 pant to a size 2, and lost all of her hair. A few months into treatment I took the initiative to ask my mom a question that had been burdening my mind; "Are you afraid to die?" I asked her. She calmly looked at me and told me that she wasn't. She said she knew Jesus and He knew her. She understood that God's sovereignty reigned and yet evil as a result of the Fall was causing her body to degenerate. The reality of cancer reveals to all of us, this is not how life ought to have been. My mom chose to trust God through her sickness. She affirmed me that she did not want to die, and that she would fight for her life, and she trusted the Lord to take care of her, me, my siblings, and my dad – regardless of what happened to her. I walked out of that room encouraged and challenged; I realized that I didn't know that God. Though I had professed Him as my Savior when I was younger, I did not know Him like my mom did, I did not trust Him with my life like she did. Soon after that conversation, I began taking personal steps towards making my faith my own; reading Scripture for insight and hope, feeling conviction, and contemplating life in Christ. This deeper seeking to know God personally affected the trajectory of my life.

Nine months after my question, my mom received a clean bill of health, and is now 28 years in remission. I'm thankful that this is my mom's story, and it also has troubled me. It troubled me because, as you might too, know others who didn't "survive" their cancer diagnosis. I don't know why some survive and some don't, it saddens me that we lose loved ones on this side of heaven; and yet, that's where God's redeeming second order story gives hope to our hurts and hang ups. While we experience death and decay on this side of Heaven, through Christ we have the promise of eternity. Spiritually speaking, Jesus wants us to cross from death to life on this side of heaven too.

My mom didn't get well by being delivered *from* the malignant condition of cancer, she got well and was delivered by going *through* cancer. It was not enough for my mom to accept that she had a malignant condition, and just show up at the doctor's office and do nothing about it. She had to be willing to accept her condition, and yield to the treatment plan to treat her malignancy. The same is true for our spiritual condition. We all have a malignant diagnosis of Sin. We can accept that condition and choose not to do anything about it; or we can accept that condition and yield to the treatment plan. This acceptance affects the trajectory of our life. Just like my mom needing to receive chemotherapy to kill off the inwardly foul malignant cancer in her body, we too need to receive a powerful treatment to kill off the inwardly foul malignant condition of Sin in our bodies. Jesus and His Holy

Spirit are the cure and the treatment plan for our sin. When we accept Christ as our Savior, He permeates our heart, the wellspring of our entire person. His Holy Spirit is activated in our life to help us live into God's story, bringing us from death to life in Christ, affecting the trajectory of our eternity and our everyday living.

Read Romans 10:9-13

- What are we to believe, and what are we to confess?

Read Romans 6:11-14

- What are we being brought from?

Read Romans 5:1-5, and 5:10-11

- What has God poured out into our hearts and how?

The word 'heart' in Greek in this passage means the center, the seat of the spiritual life. In Hebrew, it means wellspring. The heart is our wellspring, it is where all of our affections, emotions, thoughts, desires, appetites, motivations, courage, and passions spring forth from. When we accept Jesus into our hearts, we are inviting Him to permeate our wellspring which will impact the inmost part of everything in us.

Read Psalm 4: 7-8

- What does the Psalmist say the Lord filled his heart with, and what does he experience as a result?

The word 'peace' in verse eight means "without anxiety." When we invite the Lord into our personal narratives, into our life; he provides for us greater joy, peace and contentment.

Day 5, The Cool Down: Our Condition

Spend a few moments journaling, exhale and stretch out your thoughts on paper.

- How does understanding our need for Christ influence how you live? What do you feel/think as you see that the Lord desires to help us be healed from our malignant condition of Sin?

- How has the enemy deceived you from trusting Jesus wholeheartedly?
- "Are you fighting a "half-hearted battle, against a whole-hearted enemy?"[8]

This is an important question to ask ourselves, and is one that I heard Christine Caine ask in her Unashamed study. We are up against an enemy that is out to rob, kill, and destroy. It does not take more than a few seconds to read through the headlines streaming across our screens to know that there are bad things happening in our world. It's scary, but we don't have to be captives to that narrative and remain stuck in the bondage of sin and fear. Instead, we can join God in His story and join Him in His narrative of restoration, reconciliation, and redemption.

Regardless of where you are in your faith right now, I want to invite you in this moment to invite Christ into your life by inviting Him into your heart – the wellspring of your being that includes your thoughts, your fears, your hopes, and your dreams.

> "For it is with your heart that you believe and are justified, and it is with your mouth that you profess your faith and are saved." Romans 10:10

This may have been the first time you have read something like this, and you're desiring to make a decision in trusting Jesus as your Savior. In Acts 2, Peter shares the gospel and it says people were "cut to the heart," when they heard it, and they wanted to know what they were to do next. First, like them, you can privately, right where you are right now, ask Jesus to come into your life. Tell him how you recognize that your sinful condition is malignant and that you want His healing power to transform your sinful condition into righteousness. Ask Him to permeate your heart, your wellspring to positively impact the inmost part of everything about you. Ask Jesus to refresh you, and to help you walk away from living in the kingdom of sin, and into restoration of new creation through Him. After you have done that, read this prayer:

Imagine I am sitting with you, (I wish I were there in person), but for now, through the Holy Spirit, let me pray over you: "Lord Jesus, I lift this beloved child of God to you. You adore them, and you have been pursuing them with all Your Being. You have been jealous for them, desiring to have a personal relationship with them that sets them free. Thank you, Jesus, for your atonement, dying for our sin and reconciling us back to God.Thank you, Jesus, for reconciling us and justifying us by what you did on that Cross, and not by anything we could or couldn't do. Thank you Lord that you separate our who from our do, that you see us for Whose we are, and that is Yours. You created us and our innermost parts. Lord, I ask that you help this amazing sister/brother who is reading this, to walk out their days in your story, God. Help them to live into their God given capacity for your Glory Jesus. May this amazing sister/brother know how much you love them, and help them Lord to maximize their days, and be a signpost to you Jesus. Set them free from anxiety. Help them to take their thoughts captive in the knowledge of Christ. Father God, author their story with redemption, reconciliation, restoration, and healing. I love you Lord, thank you for changing my life and affecting my eternal trajectory. Thank you for allowing us to be an Ambassador for you. I am so thankful for this sister/brother and their courage to say yes to You! May the trajectory of their life in you be full of rich blessings in growing to know you and trust you more deeply Lord. I ask all this in Jesus name, Amen."

(If you asked Jesus to affect your life or recommit your life to Christ; I would love to celebrate that with you! Please send me a direct message on Instagram theobs_squad)

> [20] "For no matter how many promises God has made, they are "Yes" in Christ. And so through him the "Amen" is spoken by us to the glory of God. [21] Now it is God who makes both us and you stand firm in Christ. He anointed us, [22] set his seal of ownership on us, and put his Spirit in our

hearts as a deposit, guaranteeing what is to come." 2 Corinthians 1:20-22

As you close out today, reflect with God. What are you feeling? What are you desiring? What do you need from God? Close in prayer, and rest in knowing He loves you.

Day 6 | The Training Ground: A Private Yes

If yesterday was a day that you marked as saying a private yes to Jesus to help you live out your life, please imagine me right now giving you a high five and a side hug with a huge grin on my face smiling at you! This is honestly the most important and liberating decision you could make in your life! I am so excited for you!!!

I will never forget the day my husband proposed to me. We met while both playing professional soccer for the Christian soccer organization I mentioned earlier. During our dating time, we were growing in knowing more about one another and we liked each other. As we grew in trusting each other and desiring to spend time together, we each were able to say a private yes in our own heart that claimed the choice to want to do life with each other for the rest of our living days. Eventually this led to a marriage proposal. My husband pursued me, and offered me an invitation to do life with him. When he proposed, he didn't look at me and ask if I would marry him, he looked at me and asked if I would spend the rest of his life with him, to which I said yes. I think this is a fitting metaphor for what Jesus is doing with each of us. He is pursuing you. He desires to be known by you, and for you to allow Him to know you. As you do this, a relationship is developed, and He invites you to spend the rest of His days with Him. This is a private invitation between you and Him, and a private yes you get to make. Twenty years ago, that private yes for me to my husband, was a yes to everything that married life would offer. A yes to future children, a yes to growing old together, a yes to life's hurts & hang ups, and yes to life's highs and lows. That private yes was my commitment to all of it ahead of time. Like most proposals, a ceremony follows, and we stand before a bunch of friends and family who have been invited to celebrate with us the private yes we had made to one another days, weeks, months, years before that wedding day. This celebration is before witnesses that are in support of seeing the two of you live out the rest of your days together. That wedding day is about two people becoming one, and identifying as being each other's life partner. Spiritually speaking, a wedding day can be like a metaphor for the public celebration that baptism represents. Baptism is one of two sacred acts we can participate in, in the Kingdom of God. Baptism is a rite of entry, not an ending point. Baptism is a public celebration of the private yes between you and Jesus, and it is an important follow through in your faith in Christ.

On my wedding day, I remember when the pastor asked my husband and I to turn and face the people whom we had invited to our wedding. He asked us to look at them and to remember that moment years down the road, "for these are the people who are cheering you on, and are for you," he said. That wedding day was the day my identity shifted. I took on my husband's last name, I was now his, and he was mine. Spiritually speaking, this is significant for us in baptism too. Baptism marks the day you said Yes to Jesus publically. Your identity supernaturally shifts, you are His bride, you have taken on His name, and you can be secure in knowing Jesus will be faithful to you for all of His days.

In your own Bible, look up and read Genesis 1:1-4

- Who was hovering over the water?

John 3:5-8 from the Message version says,

Jesus said, "You're not listening. Let me say it again. Unless a person submits to this original creation—the 'wind-hovering-over-the-water' creation, the invisible moving the visible, a baptism into a new life—it's not possible to enter God's kingdom. When you look at a baby, it's just that: a body you can look at and touch. But the person who takes shape within is formed by something you can't see and touch—the Spirit— and becomes a living spirit.

7-8 "So don't be so surprised when I tell you that you have to be 'born from above'—out of this world, so to speak. You know well enough how the wind blows this way and that. You hear it rustling through the trees, but you have no idea where it comes from or where it's headed next. That's the way it is with everyone 'born from above' by the wind of God, the Spirit of God."

In your own Bible, look up and read John 1:29-34

- What stands out to you in this passage?

The word for spirit in the passages read above in John is "pneuma," which is Greek for spirit, wind, or breath. The word for spirit in Genesis 1:2 is "ruach," which is Hebrew for spirit, wind, or breath. The same Spirit of God that hovered and activated life into being in Genesis is the same energy source willing to breathe new life into us daily. God desires to usher light into our lives and illuminate His kingdom in our everyday living.

- How does this truth make you feel?

In Isaiah 54:5 we read,

For your Maker is your husband—
the Lord Almighty is his name—
the Holy One of Israel is your Redeemer;
he is called the God of all the earth.

- What stands out to you about this verse?

In a nutshell, this passage is illuminating for us that God is our Maker, our creator, and His son Jesus is our Redeemer. His Holy Spirit is active and willing to breathe new life into us and our journey. This Trinitarian fellowship of the Father, Son, and Holy Spirit is faithful to His created. The invitation to do life with God is extended to all people. The question is, are we willing to fully receive His proposal and say yes to doing life with Him for the remainder of His days?

The Cool Down, Day 6: A Private Yes

Spend a few moments journaling, exhale and stretch out your thoughts on paper.

- How does understanding this encourage you in baptism? Challenge you?
- If you have been baptized, what was special about it for you?
- If you haven't been baptized, how come?
- Take a moment to close in prayer. Share with Jesus what is stirring in your heart and mind.

Day 7 | The Training Ground: An Act of Obedience

When I was seven years old, I was baptized. While I knew then that it was a special thing, I had not fully comprehended why it was significant, and liberating. Eleven years went by, and I recommitted a private yes to Jesus when I was eighteen years old. As life happened and I was still straddling life between the kingdom of sin and the kingdom of God; I grew in knowing the

Lord more and more. When I was thirty years old, I could not deny the tugging on my heart to follow through in baptism as an adult. Spiritually speaking, it was not something I had to do, it was something I was invited to do, and I realized it was an act of obedience to follow through in doing it. I could not deny the tug on my soul to be baptized, although I personally denied the invitation many times. I realized later that Jesus didn't want something from me, He wanted something *for* me! Perhaps you can resonate with this tugging on your heart?

Let's be honest, getting baptized may just sound really intimidating, maybe you're embarrassed that you haven't been baptized yet? Or you have been baptized, but you didn't realize its impotence then, like you do now. Perhaps you were a baby or a child and were blessed by your parents faith for you. Maybe it's an endeavor that sounds neat, but you just don't want to get wet? I get it, because I felt all of those things too. I was thirty years old, a mother of two and mentoring college girls, and leading a Bible study. The tug on my heart grew increasingly stronger month after month, pushing it down and denying the tug, because quite honestly, I was prideful. "I didn't need to do that, Jesus knows I said that private yes." But let me ask you this, what if, after my husband had proposed, he told me, "Hey you know I love you, I pick you, but let's not have a wedding, you know you're important to me. You know I have said yes to you." Do you think I would question his commitment to me? Do you think I would question why He didn't want to publicly celebrate the private yes we made to one another? Do you think I would question our vulnerability to the commitment we made? Would I feel as compelled and committed down the road without that public follow through?

- If this were you and your person, how would you feel?
- How do you think Jesus feels if we intentionally reject the invitation of baptism?

Jesus knows that the enemy is out to rob, kill and destroy, John 10:10 states this. Alternatively, Jesus came to give us abundant life. In Greek, abundant is *perissos*, and means "all-around, excess; more than expected.[9] Baptism is a rite of entry, a follow through that adds blessing to abundance in Christ.

- Is being baptized something you desire in your life?
- If you have not been baptized, what is keeping you from choosing it, or living into it?

The physical act of baptism is very symbolic. Jesus was baptized in water, full immersion. This was modeling for people His yielding and participation in God's mission. As we have already unpacked, it was Jesus' work on the Cross that justifies us when we trust in faith in Christ's death and resurrection on our behalf. Baptism is a follow through in our freewill that is an act of obedience with sincere repentance for our sinful nature. The water represents being washed clean of our sin. When we are immersed in the water, we are laying down our old life (our wrong being in our sinful nature) and being brought forth out of the water, cleansed from our Sin, and birthed into the new life with Christ. This is symbolic to Jesus being buried in the tomb for our sin, and then being resurrected in New Life for our redemption. We need to be baptized not for Jesus' sake, but for our own. It's a physical follow through in laying down our sinful life and being raised to New Life in Christ.

> "Baptism – Throbs with significance, obedience to turn away from yourself focus, and enter into God's focus. Our opportunity to participate in Jesus' death, resurrection, and life; baptism as participation – not obligation. An amazing invitation."[10]

Read John 1:29-34

- Who was to be revealed to Israel? What does John testify here?

When we enter into a covenant relationship with Jesus, we become a living vessel for Jesus to be revealed through, to all the nations. Baptism is supernatural in that it affirms for us that we are His and that He is in us. It is an activating step of obedience that provides for us confidence, an access to participate in the abundant life of Christ.

Read Acts 2:32-39

- What did Peter want to make clear about Jesus in verse 36?
- What was the result of the people when they heard that "this Jesus" whom their culture had crucified was both Lord and Christ?
- What was Peter's reply to the people who asked what they should do?
- What would the people be given as a gift for their follow through in baptism?
- Who else will benefit from your decision to repent and be baptized?

To repent means to change one's mind or purpose, to "think differently after."[11] When we experience the need to change, the choice to go towards that change is repentance. When we realize the need we have for Christ, we are to confess what has kept us from walking with Him, and repent, changing direction from walking in our way and instead walk in His way. This is a trajectory game changer. In our default sinful nature, this is not always easy or a desire, but it is an act of obedience to repent and it leads to blessing.

The Cool Down, Day 7: An Act of Obedience

Spend a few moments journaling, exhale and stretch out your thoughts on paper.

- If you have been baptized, take a few minutes to write out why you did it, and why it mattered to you. Imagine you're sharing with a friend who asked you why you got baptized. Be authentic and honest in your response.
- If you have not been baptized, or you were baptized when you were a baby or a child, is it something you want to do now? Or feel like you need to do it? If so, write out why you feel this way, and reach out to a friend, a campus ministry,

a church, or someone who can help you in your faith journey. Tell them about desiring to be baptized, and ask them to help you to be accountable in following through in doing it. Remember, this is a step that is celebrated, it's an entry point, and Jesus welcomes you just as you are.

- If you don't think you're ready to be baptized, take a moment to reflect why you feel this way and invite God into the conversation with you.
- Take a few moments to close in prayer. Share with Jesus what is stirring in your heart and mind. Invite Him to help you trust Him more and more. He desires to help you walk in the trajectory of life that leads to knowing Him more deeply, and becoming all that you can be in Christ.

PART 3

Participating in the life of God

Theosis is a theological word that means participating in the life of God. This is significant to both our personal first order story, and the redeeming second order story that God calls us to live into through Christ. As the church (the body of Christ), we need to embrace participating in the life of God in our everyday lives. This is significant for us as Christ followers to understand in our identity. The church, which includes every human around the world that is a Christ follower, is an instrument for *missio Dei, The Mission of God.* Understanding our identity in Christ and the role we are called to play within

God's story shapes how we live in the world. If we don't find our role within God's story, we will find a role within a story our culture offers us, which is influenced by the kingdom of sin. The body of Christ is called to be a critical participant in its cultural setting, a "come and join us people" operating in the tension of living in the world and not being of the world. The first century church we read about in the New Testament began to understand their identity shaped by encountering Jesus and God's redeeming story, living as *paroikoi*, "resident aliens" in a culture ruled by the Roman kingdom. As the early church matured in their faith, they began to understand their role and the alternative story they were to live into, they knew they were called to make the Kingdom of God known. Sharing the redemptive good news of what God has done for the world in Jesus was the task of the church, which is still true to the body of Christ today. Like Jesus, we are called to live in the world, for the sake of the world.

In our personal first order stories, we can trust that God is working in us, *so that* we will want to do, and be able to do what pleases Him.[12] God is working in and through his creation to effect change, providing saving restorative justice. The mission of God is universal, and God's people are to be a "so that" people, *so that* they might know God's salvation and invite all nations into it. The people of God are to be countercultural, and a distinctive people displaying an attractive lifestyle to God's glory before the surrounding nations. This is why our personal first order story and how we engage living in this world matters. When our personal narratives become united with God's narrative we become evident living letters written with the Spirit. Our life in Christ activated by the Holy Spirit shifts our trajectory and affects others too. I believe that God is beckoning us into a greater story that helps us not only frame our personal story, but empowers our story to impact the world through Him. God has created us for purpose, gifting us with specific experiences, gifts, talents, passions, personality, and pursuits that are unique to each of our personal narratives. As I have understood Theosis, participating in the life of God, the Gospel itself is a powerful word of transformation. God's invitation to us through the good news of Jesus comes with a Spirit-enabling power indwelling humans to be transformed in mind, word, and deed. God is working in and through his creation to effect change, providing saving restorative justice. This is our purpose in God's mission as Christ followers. As we (the church) embody the gospel, and live out the story of redemption through Christ in our daily lives; others will be impacted by God. This is a trajectory game changer for others! The good news of Jesus Christ justifying us as righteous by His work on the cross, and redeeming creation to order, our personal stories become a Living letter written by His Holy Spirit, inviting others into His story.

Day 8 | The Training Ground: Living Letters

Read 2 Corinthians 3: 2-6,

> "You yourselves are our letter, written on our hearts, known and read by everyone. You show that you are Christ's letter, delivered by us, not written with ink but

with the Spirit of the living God — not on tablets of stone but on tablets of human hearts. Such is the confidence we have through Christ before God. It is not that we are competent in ourselves to claim anything as coming from ourselves, but our adequacy is from God. He has made us competent to be ministers of a new covenant, not of the letter, but of the Spirit. For the letter kills, but the spirit gives life."

This is the language of our first order stories being framed within God's second order story. Participating in the life of God, yielding to the Spirit-enabling power indwelling humans to be transformed in mind, word, and deed is counter cultural, and it is missional. It's how Jesus lived His incarnate life on Earth. Living this way has an impact amidst a culture when people see the life and love of Christ lived out in our personal first order stories.

- How does it make you feel that God is desiring to tell the world about Him through your personal everyday life?
- How does it make you feel to know that God's Holy Spirit gives life, and He wants to do that in and through you for the sake of the world?

Our personal life story is important, and it tells a story whether we like what it says or not. Our life's stories are letters written for others to read as we invite them to know us. The Living Letter written by the Spirit of God in your life is for others to read and meet Jesus in and through your personal life story. The following is a time-line, a life timeline for you to note milestones or events in your life that impacted you. Feel free to note more if you like. As an example, I have provided mine:

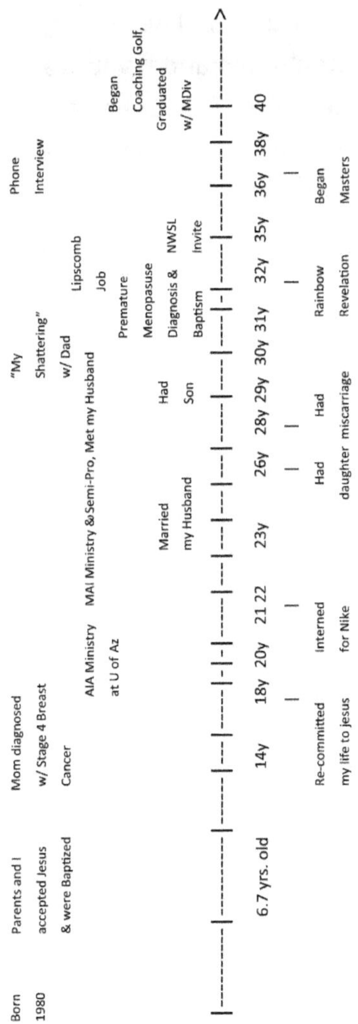

Above the timeline (left to right):

- Born 1980
- Parents and I accepted Jesus & were Baptized
- Mom diagnosed w/ Stage 4 Breast Cancer
- AIA Ministry at U of Az
- MAI Ministry & Semi-Pro, Met my Husband
- Married my Husband
- Had Son
- "My Shattering" w/ Dad
- Premature Menopasuse Diagnosis & Baptism
- Lipscomb Job
- NWSL Invite
- Phone Interview
- Began Coaching Golf, Graduated w/ MDiv

Timeline:

|------------|-----------|------|---|-----|-|-|-----|---|---|---|---|-----|----|----|-|-----|-----|----|---|--------->

Ages along the timeline:

6.7 yrs. old   14y   18y   20y   21 22   23y   26y   28y   29y   30y   31y   32y   35y   36y   38y   40

Below the timeline:

- Re-committed my life to jesus
- Interned for Nike
- Had daughter
- Had miscarriage
- Rainbow Revelation
- Began Masters

Below is your timeline, you get to decide what is written down and if you want to share it with someone else. This exercise is to help you identify events in your life that have affected you.

- After you have written your timeline out, look it over and see what themes you notice. Are there things that have a common consistency? These could be related to moving, death, celebrations, spiritual milestones, education, relationships, new births, etc.

- What do you notice when you look at your timeline? What do you feel as you look at your timeline?

- Spend some time journaling, lots of thoughts and emotions can be stirred in doing this; and getting them out of our head and on to paper can be very therapeutic and beneficial to your wellness. Remember that Jesus knows you better than you know yourself, and He loves you unconditionally. If there are areas that are painful or embarrassing as you look at your timeline, ask Jesus to help you heal from them. Ask Jesus to redeem what has been lost and broken. Ask Jesus to help you feel His love for you, and empower your life through Him.

The Cool Down, Day 8: Living Letters

Spend a few moments journaling, exhale and stretch out your thoughts on paper.

In my master's course work, I have studied theology, counseling, and spiritual direction. As you are wrapping up your timeline and reflecting, if this exercise stirs some emotions up for you, I encourage you to connect with a trusted Christian counselor or a Christian spiritual director. Processing through our story is important, and it can be very life giving, but often not without facing some hurts and hang ups. There is no shame in needing to work through things that have left us feeling broken, lost, stuck, and confused. Satan wants to keep our shame, pain, and confusion in darkness, leaving us in bondage and isolation. God desires to redeem, heal, and reconcile the chaos that sin causes in our life. Jesus desires us to live in the light of Him with liberty, peace and dignity. What follows are a few verses that highlight some truths about God.

"I have come into the world as a light, so that no one who believes in me should stay in darkness." John 12:46

"Now the Lord is the Spirit, and where the Spirit of the Lord is, there is freedom." 2 Corinthians 3:17

"Peace I leave with you. My peace I give to you. I do not give to you as the world gives. Don't let your heart be troubled or fearful." John 14:27

"The Lord your God is among you, a warrior who saves. He will rejoice over you with gladness. He will be quiet in his love. He will delight in you with singing." Zephaniah 3:17

Take a few moments to close in prayer. Invite Jesus into what you are feeling. Name to Him what is hurting. Name to Him what is confusing. Name to Him what you desire. Name to Him what you need. Ask Him for His guidance. After naming everything you need to exhale, sit in silence for a moment. Is there anything the Lord wants to say or encourage for you? Be still and rest in silence with Him. Listen. What are you sensing? Note it and ask the Lord to strengthen your faith.

Day 9 | The Training Ground: Sitting with Jesus

In the last exercise you looked at your life timeline and identified significant events that impacted your life story, your point of view, and your faith. Perhaps some things were illuminated for you. Before you read further, pray over what is stirred in you with what you saw or learned, or realized by doing the timeline exercise. Invite Jesus into what your feeling:

- To begin today, write the following statement and identify what you are feeling and desiring: "Jesus, I come to you feeling…" (write out what you are feeling). Next, write the following statement and identify what you desire from Jesus. "Jesus, I desire from you… (write what you desire from Him).

- As an example: "Jesus I come to you feeling tired, overwhelmed, and uncertain of how you can redeem parts of my story. Jesus I desire from you peace, wholeness, reconciliation and redemption."

After naming what you're feeling and desiring, imagine Jesus sitting with you. What is He wearing? How is He sitting with you? Where is He sitting? Allow yourself to rest in His presence. Note what you are feeling.

Using our imagination is an action that allows our minds to be creative. Our imagination allows us to form mental images to help us wholly perceive reality. God has gifted us with an imagination. Choosing to use our imagination to picture Jesus in our reality can connect us with Him in deep ways and help us experience His presence.

In this next passage of Scripture read, I want you to read it imagining the situation of Jesus encountering and interacting with the people in the passage. Take note of what you notice and what stands out to you in the following verses:

Read Mark 8:22-26

- What stands out to you in these verses?
- What are you curious about?
- How do you imagine Jesus with this blind man?
- How do you imagine the blind man felt?
- What stands out to you about Jesus?

We may not always understand Jesus and His activity. Something that stood out to me was how Jesus first took the blind man's hand and led him away from everyone. Almost like Jesus wanted the man to know He saw him and led him to be one on one with Him. Jesus then spits and places His hands on the man. This is odd in our culture, but something that stands out to me is the healing power of Jesus' DNA. His spit carries His DNA and is medicinal when Jesus chooses to lay His hands on the man's eyes and provides sight for the blind man.

- Are there wounds or metaphorical blindness in your life that needs Jesus' healing touch?

The Cool Down, Day 9: Sitting with Jesus

Imagine Jesus sitting with you. Close your eyes and imagine Him taking you by the hand and guiding you to a quiet place. Contemplate and journal as you reflect over the following questions:

- Jesus is with you, what do you see?
- Where is He with you?
- What is His posture like?
- What do you sense He wants you to know?
- How are you experiencing Jesus' presence right now?
- Is there anything you want to tell Jesus or ask of Jesus? If so, tell Him.
- Is there anything Jesus wants to say to you?

Pause in silence, and listen. Write down what you are feeling, sensing, seeing, and hearing.

After you reflect over the questions, close in prayer. Ask Jesus to help you see as He sees. Ask Jesus to heal any blindness you might have spiritually, figuratively, and literally.

Thank Jesus for being near and desiring to sit with you. Remember that our imagination is a gift from God. Encountering Jesus in prayer can have real life impact on our hearts and minds. Rest in Him and close in prayer as you feel led.

Day 10 | The Training Ground: Agents of God

Jesus wants to activate your life, while actively living alongside you, and in you through His Holy Spirit. As we live into God's story, we are activated by the Holy Spirit to become agents of God. The church is to participate in the life of God to be agents of enabling others to participate in the mission of God by becoming the gospel of peace.[13] It is imperative that our daily living is connected to the internal life of the Holy Spirit; embracing the life of peace, love, and righteousness in Christ, so that we can embody a true witness to the world. This is a trajectory game changer that will have an eternal impact for you and all who are impacted by Christ through your life.

Read 1 Corinthians 15:10

- God's grace was not without ____________.

The following Scripture passage is from the Amplified[14] Bible translation. This is a letter (an epistle) written to the Philippians by the Apostle Paul while he was in prison. He is writing a letter with a pastoral heart to exhort and encourage the Philippian church:

[12] So then, my dear ones, just as you have always obeyed [my instructions with enthusiasm], not only in my presence, but now much more in my absence, continue to work out your salvation [that is, cultivate it, bring it to full effect, actively pursue spiritual maturity] with awe-inspired fear and trembling [using serious

caution and critical self-evaluation to avoid anything that might offend God or discredit the name of Christ]. [13] For it is [not your strength, but it is] [a]God who is effectively at work in you, both to will and to work [that is, strengthening, energizing, and creating in you the longing and the ability to fulfill your purpose] for His good pleasure. (Philippians 2:12-13)

- What most strikes you about this passage? What stood out to you?

Read John 1:38

- What do they call Jesus, and what does that title mean?
- When you go to a class, practice, or some work-related seminar, who is responsible to teach the student, or run the training session?

When I attend class, if my teacher is not prepared, I am not going to get a lot out of it. Same is true if I show up to class and not apply myself in listening and absorbing the lesson. I will never forget one time I went to the gym and I chose to have a casual workout. I got on an exercise bike and pedaled at leisure for thirty minutes. While I got a little something out of it, I was quite annoyed with myself at the end when I looked at the digital stats on the bike. I realized when looking at my heart rate and my calorie burn, I did not maximize my thirty minutes to its fullest potential, in some regard, I wasted my time. I knew this because usually I would run on the treadmill, at the end of 30 minutes as all the stats read out, I was much sweatier, out of breath, and my calories burned were significantly higher, even if I only did fifteen minutes on the treadmill, it far exceeded my casual thirty minutes on the bike that one day. As I sat there debating if I do another 15-30 mins on the bike, I realized this had been metaphorical to my spiritual growth during that season in my life. Spiritually speaking, for a long time, I coasted. I just pedaled at leisure, I attended church at a casual level. Just enough to get a little out of it, but not everything out of it. Like that gym time, when I realized this,

I was annoyed with myself for forfeiting the opportunity to really apply myself in my personal walk with Jesus. I realized I wanted to maximize my training and get the most out of my time.

Read the following verses:

1 Timothy 4:8

"For physical training is of some value, but godliness has value for all things, holding promise for both the present life And the life to come."

In the Greek language of 1 Timothy 4:8, the word "godliness" means to have piety (reverence) towards God. In our Fallen human condition, we need help to train our hearts and minds to respond in life with reverence towards God in all things.

2 Timothy 3:16-17

"All Scripture is God-breathed and is useful for teaching, rebuking, correcting and training in righteousness, [17] so that the servant of God[a] may be thoroughly equipped for every good work."

As an athlete and a coach, I understand the value in studying the play book, considering the opponent, and memorizing plays to help us prepare for the match ahead. For us to grow in godliness, we need to study the Word of God and be immersed in a community with others pursuing godliness. We need to allow Scripture to inform our understanding of God's story and mission. We need to do life in community with fellow Christ followers to help us sharpen one another and grow in godliness (reverence for God), and in compassion to love others well.

Read Philippians 2:13 from the Amplified[15] Bible translation:

[13] For it is [not your strength, but it is] [a] God who is effectively at work in you, both to will and to work [that is, strengthening, energizing, and creating in you the

longing and the ability to fulfill your pur-
pose] for His good pleasure.

- Who is working in us?
- Why is He working in us?

In a nutshell, God is working in you, *so that,* you will want to do, and be able to do what pleases Him. It is God, like the teacher prepared for class, that is responsible to bring the lesson to the learning environment, but in our freewill, just like a student attending class, or a person doing a workout, we are responsible to lean in and apply ourselves to get the most out of it.

- Have you ever been able to do something, but you just didn't want to?
- Or perhaps you were really wanting to do something, but you just weren't able to yet?

This is what God is about, working in us *so that* we will both *want to* and *be able to* fulfill our purposes that pleases Him. I will never for-get the day my son, who was only seven years old at the time, offered to drive the car for me from the front of the house to the back. God bless Him, I love his confidence. My son honestly believed that he was able to drive our SUV fifty feet around the back corner of our house. As I thanked him for offering and wanting to help me, I had to explain that he was not yet able to do that. As these words came out of my mouth, I heard an inner whisper from the Holy Spirit to me; He said, "Shannon, this is like you, there are things you are confident to do, but not yet able to." Oh man, I felt conviction. The Lord was right. How often have I had the confidence to say "I want to," but I was not yet able to. Or times when God has said, "you're able to," and I have responded with, "I don't want to." Thankfully, we can rest in knowing that God is at work in us. May we be prayerful and ask the Lord to help us maximize our days for His glory, and grow in godliness so that we will want to do and be able to do the things that please Him.

Day 10, The Cool Down: Agents of God

Spend a few moments in reflection think-ing about things you could do, but don't want to; and with that, the things you can't do, but want to. Exhale and stretch out your thoughts on paper before God.

- If the above section resonates for you, confess to the Lord through prayer what has convicted you, ask the Lord to help you repent of it, and to help you long for and have the ability for your purpose that pleases Him. Ask the Lord to help you grow in godliness and walk in His ways. Ask Him to help you live into His story and have the trajectory of your life influence others to also become a "so that" person expanding God's Kingdom for His glory. Close in prayer as you feel led.

Day 11 | The Training Ground: A Credible Commentary

I believe the world we live in is in exile to the original created order God had intended for us before the Fall. Our beautiful earth and its ordered system has been affected by the Fall, where the kingdom of sin has caused corruption, brokenness, sickness, injustice, and pain. Thankfully, the kingdom of sin we live in is not eternal, and only temporary.

I believe each person in Christ is on an "exodus" journey. Like the Israelites, as we pursue life with God in trajectory for His Promise Land, we too are leaving bondage, being weaned from the familiar worldly culture, and being beckoned to trust in the Lord as He makes Himself known in our everyday life. The same purpose of the early church in Acts, is the same for the church today. We as the global body of Christ are to be a light to the nations; living into a redeemed order bringing forth hope and purpose amidst a lost and wounded culture. Throughout New Testament Scripture, Paul offers truths and pastoral guidance that provides clarity for the church not to assimilate or fearfully abandon what the Lord called the body of Christ to represent. Paul's letters in the New Testament are to help Christ followers understand the master story of God's mission (to redeem His creation), both in the narrative of Christ and the narrative of the church. Paul wanted to help Christ followers understand and embrace the love of Christ, living as a contrasting community amidst their culture. Paul exhorts the church to continue to proclaim the gospel with their lives and their lips, living out the Good News of Jesus Christ in servanthood, to continue becoming and telling the story of Christ despite persecution.[16] Paul wants the church to defend and be a *credible commentary* on the story that narrates the mission of God.

Read Ezekiel 36: 19-26

- At the end of verse 23, who does the Lord want to show Himself holy through, and why?
- In verse 25, what will God cleanse His people of?

- In verse 26, what does the Lord say He will give His people? What will he remove from us?

In this verse God is making it clear that He is going to do something new, not for our sake, but for His, to redeem the world. We are blessed in the process of Him doing this; He wants us to get in on His mission. He wants us to be agents for Him to operate in and through to reconcile His creation back to wholeness and fellowship. In Ezekiel 36:24-27 we see the four[17] elements of the promised restoration in the Old Testament now available to us through Christ:

(1) The return of exiles: His people who have had broken relationship and fellowship with God can now return to God through Christ's restorative obedience on the Cross.
(2) We are cleansed from sin through baptism.
(3) He renews our heart, our soul, and our comprehending mind.

(4) He enables us to live by God's Spirit to live God's way.

Through Christ, the trajectory of our lives is impacted. Choosing to live into His story and become a credible commentary on the Good News of Jesus Christ will also impact the trajectory of other lives.

The Cool Down, Day, 11: A Credible Commentary

Spend some time reflecting and stretching out your thoughts.

- Understanding the invitation to be an agent for God, how can you in your everyday personal life live as a credible commentary to God's story of restoration? How might your story of restoration and redemption through Christ affect your surrounding culture?
- How does this affect how you do things? In your home life? In your workplace? If you are on a team, how does this

shape and frame how you approach, behave, and pursue sport? As a credible commentary, like Christ, how does this shape and frame how you approach, behave, and treat other people?

- What are some areas or things that may be hindering a credible commentary of God's story in your everyday living?
- How do you want to be a Living Letter, a credible commentary of God's story as you live your life? As you train and play your sport? As you do your daily job?
- How might living as a credible commentary bless the people around you? Bless your opponents or co-workers?
  - If this brings conviction to your heart, confess with your mouth those things, and ask the Lord to help you want to do and be able to do the things that please Him for the sake of the world, and the blessing of your future family and God's Kingdom. God is for you. Your

> relationship with Him is secure in His covenant. Your fellowship with Him is deepened when you lean into Him.

Close in prayer as you feel led. Ask God to help you be and become a credible commentary of His greater story, influencing how and why you live the way you do. Ask Him to help you live in such a way that others are drawn to Him and His goodness.

Day 12 | The Training Ground: Transformation

I have a passion for transformation, and I love good design. It wasn't until my life was leveled by fatigue and sideswiped by father's sinful confession that I realized more of my design in Christ. You see, I was living out life with faith in Christ but I wasn't consciously living into His mission. I had strongholds in my life that were inhibiting me, and it wasn't until my father's personal stronghold was exposed that my life shattered and permitted the opportunity for the Holy Spirit to permeate every broken crevice and illuminate my calling. I realized my calling was to live into the mission of God, while fellowshipping with the Trinity; which is also your calling. It's every single human being's calling. How that calling looks lived out is unique in each of our personal first order stories, because every human has a life with circumstances and choices affecting how it unfolds. We all have different passions and sensitivities, and that is a good thing as the body of Christ! It's an invitation to each of us in our freewill to lean into Jesus, and accept and partner with God in His mission through our personal lives. We witness throughout all of Scripture multiple people affected by God's overarching redemptive narrative. For example, Esther's story is unique to her, Moses' story is unique to him, Paul's story is unique to him, Jesus' story is unique to him; and in that, all their stories are anchored in God's Greater Story, influencing and affecting the choices they made and how they lived out their life on earth and pursued the trajectory of God's mission for the sake of others.

During the winter of 2009 I visited my parents out west where I grew up. I had just had my second child and was exhausted. I went on a mountain trail run to clear my head. The worship song in my ear kept repeating "More of You, less of me; more of You, less of me."[18] Those lyrics became a prayer as my feet carried me off the desert trail and back onto the asphalt road leading me into the neighborhood valley. Thirty days later, my father was arrested for soliciting a prostitute. Six months later my dad sat me down and confessed his story of addiction. I remember shortly after he shared his story with me, he said, "Wow, I feel so much better." I was reeling. He made himself a sandwich and as he sat down to eat it, I stood a few feet away at my kitchen island, bewildered by what I had just learned, and questioning how the man even had an appetite at that moment; because I felt sick. As I watched him take a bite of his sandwich, I heard the Lord whisper, "Look at him." Hesitantly, I did, and as he took that bite of sandwich, the Lord whispered to me, "that is a lost little boy in need of a Savior." Now years removed, I know the Lord was showing me in that moment, how He can separate a person's "who" from their "do."[19] My dad was a sinful man, lost and in need of a Savior. That is who he was, and what he did in sin, emotionally hurt me. What followed after that day for me was a season of despair and searching. I leaned into the Word of God, and painstakingly pursued obedience and reconciliation. I prayed for the Lord to deliver me from the mess, but He made it clear He would deliver me *through* the mess. The Lord revealed to me that going *through* it will give me the tools the Lord needed me to have to help others.

In my journey over the next year, through a Bible study, the Lord revealed to me the strongholds He was breaking me free from: people pleasing, fear, worry, and self-reliance. I was on an exodus journey. It was by God's grace and mercy that He showed me the truth, and allowed me to wrestle. His Divine action in showing me *who* my father was, separated from what he *did*, was a gift. It also has humbled me as I have come to realize that God too has done this for me, He has separated my who from my do.

This has liberated me. This has helped me grasp a greater sense of who I am and grounded me in finding my identity fully in Him. My Father's sinful behavior was a shattering experience for my family. Spiritually speaking, it was a "death to life" moment in my personal first order story. Practical theologian Andrew Root defines the paradigm of the *theologia crucis* as the "death to life, life-out-of-death"[20] occurrence when we in our personal concrete experiences of God bring us from our human impossibility into God's possibility. This is part of our Theosis journey, participating in the life of God in our first order stories as we live into God's redeeming second order story.

- Looking back at your life timeline you created on Day 8, can you identify any "death to life" moments in your personal story?
- Have you ever encountered any concrete experiences of God in your life where His possibility brought

"life-out-of-death" occurrences for you or others in your personal story?

Read Jeremiah 29:11-13 from the Amplified Bible (AMP)[21]

[11] For I know the plans *and* thoughts that I have for you,' says the LORD, 'plans for peace *and* well-being and not for disaster, to give you a future and a hope. [12] Then you will call on Me and you will come and pray to Me, and I will hear [your voice] *and* I will listen to you. [13] Then [with a deep longing] you will seek Me *and* require Me [as a vital necessity] and [you will] find Me when you search for me with all your heart.

Referencing the passage of scripture above, answer the following questions:

- What are the Lord's plans and thoughts for you?
- What will God do when you call on Him and pray?

- When you do this, what does verse 13 tell you will be the result when you seek Him with all of your heart (your inner will)?

The word peace in verse 11 is *shalom* in Hebrew[22], which means completeness, soundness (safety), and friendship and covenant relationship. God desires for us to seek Him with all of our will, and in doing so, we experience security in God's story.

The Cool Down, Day 12: Transformation

God designed humankind to be in relationship with Him, to experience shalom, and walk with Him in all of our days. The worldly culture we live in has diluted this truth, and offered us a secondary story that does not even compare to the fullness of God's story. Our calling as a child of God is to continue the ministry of Jesus in all its facets acting in mercy and justice, operating with integrity, and self-giving love. We have the deep hope of God at work in us and through us to serve the unbelieving world, so that others may read a credible commentary, a Living Letter of Christ and want to get in on God's story.

- How does this make you feel?
- How did Jeremiah 29:11-13 AMP version encourage you and challenge you in your personal story?
- How has the truth of knowing God separates our who from our do, and still loves us, impact you?

Close in prayer. Tell the Lord what's stirring in your heart and mind. Invite God into your longings and convictions. Ask God to meet you where you are at in your journey of faith. Be fully honest with Him, and allow His life of love, truth, and grace, to influence how you live.

PART 4

Designed by God

I have a heart to help others unpack their personal first order story and find hope in God's redeeming second order story. As we discover our story in God's story, transformation happens. This is a trajectory game changer with an eternal impact. Life's hurts and hang-ups can inhibit and derail us from living into Christ's liberty, and get us caught up in a kingdom of sin trajectory for our life. As we feel stuck in bondage, or tarnished by trauma, Satan's lies keep us from living fully into the story of God (which is what the Enemy wants to do – keep us from all that God intends for us).

Additionally, I have a heart to help others discover how they are wired. In my experience, helping people discover their gifts, passions, values, and personality types has been important to empowering others in self-acceptance, while also encouraging them in yielding their design to the Lord. I have found that understanding how we are designed uniquely by God is beneficial in living out our first order stories intentionally. When we understand how we are wired, we can live functionally into our design.

In my undergraduate degree, I studied graphic design and illustration. In my professional design portfolio, I have designed for Nike, created professional business identities, and designed homes and environments that are intended to invite others into something greater. While interning for Nike, I grew in realizing how important functional design was to problem solving, while also being aesthetically pleasing. Nike was one of the first to begin engineering athletic shoes that had both function and appeal. Tinker Hatfield and Bill Bowerman worked to develop products that empowered and equipped athletes to achieve performance. The detail and intent behind every aspect of a Nike shoe is significant. I think this is a pretty cool analogy to what God is doing in us. He is the ultimate designer, intentionally and specifically designing His creation to have both functional and ascetic appeal; and to be utilized in achieving His mission. God is at work well ahead of time before we hit the metaphorical market. When we live into the God-given function we were designed for, it has a gathering effect, serving others as a signpost to our Creator.

God's mission is to restore His creation. In that, God is transformational and not just transactional. Ever since The Fall and sin derailing Creation, God has been at work to restore order. We, as His people, are to have an effective role in His Story. He has atoned us through Christ, and invited us to live into His redeeming story, liberating us from bondage, and transforming us through His Spirit. But, as we have been studying, if we frame this solely in terms of the world's second order story; we will fall short in our effect. Imagine if a track athlete tried to run in speed skates, or a baseball player used a badminton racket instead of a bat; the athlete (and team) would be impaired in their function and performance. Yet, every day, when we don't understand our design, our function, and the mission we are called to as a member of Christ's body, we are impaired to make the most of our days.

Victor Frankl, historic psychologist and Auschwitz Holocaust survivor, endorsed that "everyone has his own specific vocation or mission in life to carry out, a concrete assignment which demands fulfillment. Therein he cannot be replaced, nor can his life be repeated. Thus, everyone's task is as unique as is his specific opportunity to implement it."[23] Every person matters to God and each has purpose in God's story. We each have been uniquely designed by God in His image. Our gifts are what we do, our passions are where we do them, and our personality is how we do them.[24] These aspects of ourselves help to illuminate how we live into the vocation of God's story in our unique personal lives. Our unique vocation in our first order story provides for us work to be done; we have gifts, passions, and a personality that God wants to implement for His Kingdom. In so doing, it becomes a Living Letter written by God, to His Glory that not only blesses others, but you too. When we allow our first order narrative to be weaved into God's redeeming second order narrative, our lives become a signpost to Jesus, and His story empowers our unique story to the suffering world. This is part of the terms and conditions of being gathered into an eschatological people living into the missional calling of Jesus. Being born again in Christ provides for us the opportunity to live into New Creation; making choices now *so that* others will want to get in on what God is doing in and through His covenant people. We as Christ followers are to become the Gospel message, to embody the good news of Jesus Christ in our everyday living, and advance it. As we do this, we will be living into the *missio Dei*, for the sake of the world to experience the Kingdom of God both now, and when Christ returns.

Day 13 | The Training Ground: Gifts are What You Do

In Mark 12:30, Jesus says,

"Love the Lord your God with all your heart and with all your soul and with all your mind and with all your strength."

Jesus tells us to do this, which are four key parts of our human make up that we need to consciously engage. When we pursue loving God with all of our being – with our breath, our talents, our passions, and our thinking – we are maximizing the opportunity to live into the fulness of God.

Spiritual gifts are a God-given capacity to be a 10 out of 10, and to effectively impact the world by the work of the Spirit in your life. Just as a child shows the ability and potential to grow in a natural gift, the same is true for us as children of God and maturing in spiritual gifts. A child who shows an aptitude to play sports when they are young cannot perform at a professional level until they develop their strength, skills, and understanding. Same is true for us in our God given capacity. We need to lean into Jesus and allow His life and Holy Spirit to develop our spiritual giftings.

Read 1 Corinthians 12

- Why is the manifestation of the Spirit given? (see verse 7)
- How did the analogy of the one body and many parts help you understand how the many people of God have a specific role to play for the greater good of all?
- What are some gifts and/or talents you have been told you have?

The Cool Down, Day 13: Gifts Are What You Do

To learn what your spiritual gifting could be, check out the following resources and take their free assessments.[25] Each of them will guide you and offer you additional resources to flush out growing in knowing your gifts and how to develop them:

Meck Institute Spiritual Gifts
Assessment:
https://mecker.typeform.com/to/c11y32ys

Churchgrowth.org Spiritual Gifts Survey:
http://gifts.churchgrowth.org/
spiritual-gifts-survey/

Spiritual Gifts Test:
https://spiritualgiftstest.com/my-account/

When you take these assessments, answer the questions as honestly as you can. Sometimes we can feel like we need to answer a question based on what we think an answer "should" be as a Christian, but don't do that; be honest because it will produce a truer result. The assessment will give you insight to your God-given capacity and the gifts that can be developed to effectively impact the world for God's Kingdom. As a member of the body of Christ, your gifts are to help build up the Church, to offer fruit so that others can be impacted by the work of the Lord in your life.

For your cool down, take the assessments and review what each gifting is when you get your immediate results.

- After completing the assessments, write down your top three gifts and ask the Lord to grow you, and develop your gifts so that others can be built up by them. Ask the Lord to effectively use you for His glory.

1.
2.
3.

Close in prayer as you feel led. Name your gifts to the Lord and ask Him to help you utilize them for His glory and Kingdom gain. Ask the Lord to help you grow in knowing Him, and trusting Him throughout your life.

Day 14 | The Training Ground: Your Passions Are Where You Use Your Gifts

Passions are the areas that matter to you. Areas that you have holy discontent for, or areas that might make you annoyed or bother you that something needs to improve. Passions can also be things that you enjoy.

Passions can be discovered through looking at these things:

1. What are your talents? What are you naturally good at? What did you show an aptitude in as a child?
2. What bothers you? Is there an area in social justice that you have discovered really matters to you, and it bothers you when the world neglects it?
3. What did you love to do as a child?
4. What do you love to do? What comes as naturally as breathing to you?
5. What helps to motivate you to get out of bed in the morning?
6. Where are areas that you can invest your heart and time in right now that would excite you?
7. What makes you come alive when you get to do them?

The Cool Down, Day 14: Your Passions Are *Where* You Do Them

Spend some time chewing on the questions above, and seek to discover what your passions are. Your passions are areas to use your gifts. For example, I'm passionate about helping people through sports. My spiritual gifts are shepherding, leadership, teaching, and exhortation, which are utilized through coaching and mentoring student-athletes.

Colossians 3:23 says, "Whatever you do, work at it with all your heart, as working for the Lord, not for human masters,"

- How does this verse encourage you and challenge you?

Ask God to help you realize your passions and to help you utilize your gifts to serve Him and His Kingdom. Seek ways to use your gifts in these areas you're passionate about. Close in prayer as you feel led.

Day 15 | The Training Ground: Your Personality is *How* You Do Your Gifts

Our personality refers to how we think, act, and feel. Carl Jung a psychologist who developed the Analytic theory desired to help people grow in awareness and become whole. Dr. Jung discovered two psychological types that he believed were inherent tendencies in humans; we today understand and identify these types as being an introvert or extrovert. In our personality types we have rational thoughts and feelings and we make decisions through our perceptions. Embracing our personality and allowing ourselves to be authentic is liberating and life giving; it is how we are to do our gifts in our areas of passion.

There are two personality tests that we can take for free that help us discover our personality types.

- Myers-Briggs personality test was influenced by Carl Jung's work. Here is the link to take the Myer-Briggs test:

http://www.humanmetrics.com/cgi-win/
jtypes2.asp

The other test is the Enneagram, originally developed in the 4th century by the Desert Fathers who had a heart to help people grow in spiritual formation. The more aware we become of our true self the more aware we can grow in knowing ourselves and God. The Enneagram is intended through a Christian lens to help people in identifying traits and underlying compulsions that are a part of our personality type. Jokingly, I had a friend describe to me, the Myers-Briggs test is like, "Oh! This is me!" in a happy tone; and the Enneagram, in a straightforward tone is like, "oh crap, this is me." The following links are resources I personally used in reference to discovering more about personalities:

SimilarMinds.com:
http://similarminds.com/personal-
ity_test.html

Your Enneagram Coach: https://assessment.yourenneagram-coach.com/

Taking these inventory tests will be illuminating, and helpful in becoming more self-aware. Author David G. Benner says, "Still, Christian spirituality has a great deal to do with the self, not just with God. The goal of the spiritual journey is the transformation of self. As we shall see, this requires knowing both ourself and God. Both are necessary if we are to discover our true identity as those who are "in Christ" (2 Corinthians 5: 17), because the self is where we meet God. Both are also necessary if we are to live out the uniqueness of our vocation." As we grow in understanding ourselves,we also grow in knowing our Creator, which is a blessing to our relationship and fellowship with the Lord.

The Cool Down, Day 15: Your Personality Is How You Do Them

Spend some time taking these inventory's and discover more about how you are wired.

- Write down your four type Myers-Briggs personality type here:

  _______ _______ _______ _______

- What is your Enneagram number(s)?

  ____

After learning your personality types, reflect over what you learned about yourself.

- What was helpful and empowering?
- What was illuminating and challenging?

I encourage you to look deeper into some other resources to further discover how our personality can influence this world and make a Kingdom impact in your unique design by God. Please note, the Enneagram and Myers Brigg tests should never be used to judge, shame, or negatively label others or yourself. These per-sonality tests are helpful illuminators to your wiring; which can help provide steering han-dles in navigating circumstances, relationships, and choices in your life. One of the most helpful aspects of these tests are to embrace the reality that there is a kingdom of sin, and how that can influence how we live, as much as, the Kingdom of God. Discernment through Christ is needed and I encourage you to work out understanding your fleshly human nature and Christ centered nature with a Christian who is an Enneagram coach or Spiritual Director.

In my personal journey, I gained to understand that our gifts, passions, and personality illuminate how to carry out our purpose and calling; and live into God's greater story through our personal lives. As a personal example, I have learned that I am an ENFJ on Myers Briggs, and on the Enneagram I am a 2, a helper. With that, I also have learned that I have a lot of a 3 wing, and some 8 in me. This helps me to understand that I am an extroverted helper. I care to help and achieve for the sake of others. This can sound very positive, but I also have become aware that I can be tempted to please others in my self-reliance. I can seek to achieve instead of resting my worth solely in Christ and what He declares true over me. As a challenger, my 8 areas of my personality can come out more directly than I may desire when I am stressed out. Understanding this has helped to illuminate for me where my fleshly human sinfulness can get the best of me. Working through this awareness and asking God to help me live into His likeness in my wiring has been incredibly beneficial and life giving. Not just for me, but for those I am doing life with day in and day out.

As you close for the day, take a moment to reflect on all that you have discovered about yourself.

Reflect on:

- What do you ultimately desire by knowing all this about yourself?
- What do you ultimately desire for the Lord and His Kingdom and your role in His mission? What do you need from God to help you live into His design of you, for His glory?

Name your longings to the Lord in prayer. Remember that you are the only expression of Jesus Christ in the shape and being of you. Your life, passions, gifts, and personality matter to God. Ask Him to help you grow and mature in

Him. Ask Him to help you partner with Him in His mission and live into your God given design for His glory and Kingdom gain. Close in prayer as you feel led.

PART 5

Cultivating Life in View of a Telos

For the last ten years, I have had the privilege to walk with NCAA D1 student-athletes at Lipscomb University as the Director of Women's Spiritual Formation for our female athletes. I served in the capacity of spiritual direction, mentoring, and discipleship with our students. This Trajectory devotional was born out of my time with them while reflecting on missional strategy and living into God's story with my experiences, gifts, and passions. I have found that providing a framework that offers a virtuous pathway geared towards understanding our *being*, helps us refine our choices and discern our *doing*. When we pursue life with a telos (goal) in mind, we can pursue "becoming" with greater intention because we *know* the goal we are headed towards. Understanding our *being (our existence)* can help to inform us in how and what we need to do, to strive for the goals we seek to reach. Understanding our identity in God's redemptive story helps us to embrace life as we seek to grow in *knowing* Christ more deeply; which will influence our *becoming and our doing* as we seek to make the most of our days for God's glory.

Day 16 | The Training Ground: Understanding Our Being, Knowing, and Doing

As we unpacked at the start of this book, our identity is to be found in Christ and what He declares true over us. As we come to understand this, it helps us to feel liberated in our *doing*, because our doing no longer has to measure our worth in this world. When we operate from the lens of God's narrative, our doing becomes more purposeful to live into His mission. God's telos (goal) is to redeem and restore His creation. As we are part of God's creation, His goal for us includes a trajectory with liberation because we are finding our worth in His Truth and faithfulness instead of the everchanging noise of the world and our shortcomings.

- Read the following passages of Scripture, what stands out to you?

  Proverbs 16:9, "A person's heart plans his way, but the LORD determines his steps."

  Proverbs 3:5-6, "Trust in the Lord with all your heart, and do not lean on your own understanding. In all your ways acknowledge him, and he will make straight your paths."

  Psalm 119:2, "Blessed are those who keep his statutes and seek him with all their heart."

Proverbs 16:3, "Commit your work to the Lord, and your plans will be established."

Psalm 32:8, "I will instruct you and teach you in the way you should go; I will counsel you with my eye upon you."

Psalm 90:12, "Teach us to number our days, that we may gain a heart of wisdom."

Philippians 3:14, "I press on toward the goal for the prize of the upward call of God in Christ Jesus."

- What encourages you from all the passages above? What challenges you?

Earlier in this book we unpacked that the word "heart" means wellspring. The very source where your thoughts, emotions, passions, etc. spring forth from within you. Understanding this, reflect again on the passages above. How does your heart and the goals you have had, align with God's goal to do life with you and through you?

It's not wrong to desire all kinds of goals in life, but it is important to consider your motives for those goals.

- Jot down some goals for your life.
- Jot down some goals on where you would like to be a year from now.
- Jot down where you would like to be 5 years from now.
- Jot down where you would like to be 10 years from now.
  - Why do you want to achieve the above goals you have in mind?
  - How does God's goal to redeem and restore creation illuminate your purpose within your unique design?
  - How does your purpose in God's story illuminate your pursuit of being, knowing, and doing?

Day 16, The Cool Down: Understanding our Being, Knowing, and Doing

Take a moment to reflect and stretch out your thoughts. Remember that God has designed you with passions, gifts, talents, and strengths. All of which are expressed through your personality and life lived.

- Reflecting on your gifts, passions, and personality, consider what you are pursuing in life; is it in trajectory with what you want to become in Christ?
- Is what you are pursuing in life cultivating oneness with God? Why or why not?

Reflecting on these types of questions will help us to really consider the truth of our actions, behaviors, practices, habits and goals. Remember that the goal of the spiritual journey is the transformation of self in Christ, which requires knowing both our self and God. Both of which are necessary if we are to discover our true identity in Christ and live into His missional telos.

Reflect on these questions:

- Are your goals strengthened in Christ as you consider them in light of God's telos?
- Where do you feel unknown?
- Where do you need God's guidance? Where do you need His reassurance?

Close in prayer. Lift your desires and longings to God. He understands your heart. He understands the why behind your goal setting. He understands what you hope to get out of your *doing*. Commit your ways to Him and trust that He will direct your steps. Seek Him as you journey in your becoming. Trust Him in faith as you discern where to stay and where to go. It's okay if you don't have it all figured out, seek the Lord and He will walk with you along the way.

Day 17 | The Training Ground: The Virtue Model

The following virtue model, which was taught in my graduate Christian Ethics class by Dr. Lee Camp, was originally taught by Aristotle, and later modified through theologian Thomas Aquinas. Aquinus pointed out that we in our fallen sinful condition need the infusion of the Lord to be able to grow and become as we could be in God's telos.[26] The pathway of grace and truth in Christ affords us the opportunity to live as we could be. The work of Jesus on the cross and the infusion of His Holy Spirit in our lives is what affords our *being* to develop and grow in the likeness of Christ.[27] Being mindful in practicing virtues can help us cultivate our goals in life.

On the following page is the Virtue Model diagram, an illustration to highlight a pathway to becoming.

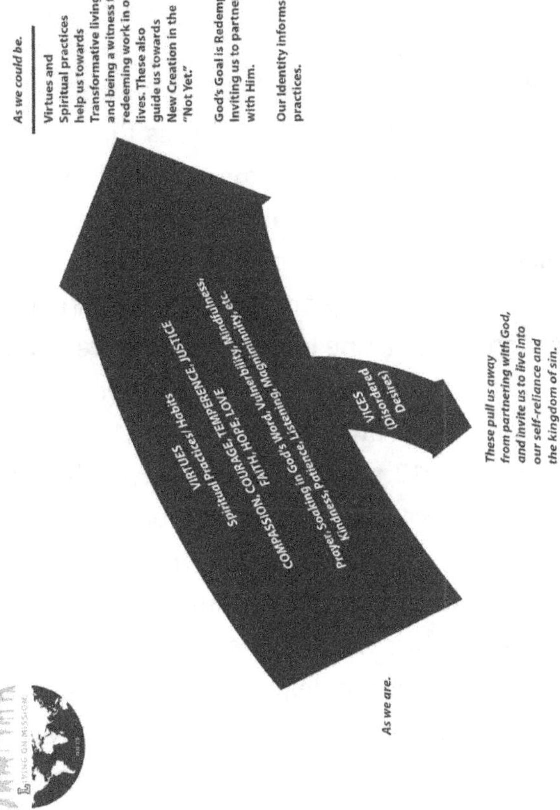

As we could be.

Virtues and
Spiritual practices
help us towards
Transformative living
and being a witness to God's
redeeming work in our
lives. These also
guide us towards
New Creation in the
"Not Yet."

God's Goal is Redemptive-
Inviting us to partner
with Him.

Our Identity informs our
practices.

VIRTUES/ Habits
Spiritual Practices: TEMPERENCE, JUSTICE
COMPASSION, COURAGE, HOPE, LOVE
FAITH, Vulnerability, Magnimininity, etc.
Prayer, Soaking in God's Word, Listening,
Kindness, Patience,

VICES
(Disordered
Desires)

These pull us away
from partnering with God,
and invite us to live Into
our self-reliance and
the kingdom of sin.

As we are.

LIVING ON MISSION

On the adjacent page, the illustrated Virtue Model identifies a trajectory. On the left side of the arrow, we read "As we are." This is where we are currently. The arrow serves as a visual pathway, a trajectory when our doing is full of virtues and spiritual practices to take us towards "As we could be." Both vices and virtues that we "do" can lead us away or towards our goals and God's telos. God's telos has an eschatological goal in mind, a final destiny for our soul and oneness with Him. In paying attention to God's redemptive goal, we can be informed and more mindful in how we choose to live and partner with God in working out our salvation.

In John 17, we read Jesus' prayer the hours before He was arrested to be crucified. Did you know Jesus prayed for you? And for everyone that would come to know Him through you? He did. With this, Jesus also specifically asked His Heavenly Father to help us *know* Him. The word *know* here in Greek means to personally learn to perceive, to come to recognize, to personally experience.[28] Jesus stated that this is eternal life:

to come to *know* Him. This is significant, and a trajectory illuminator!

> **John 17:3,** "This is eternal life: that they may know you, the only true God, and the one you have sent — Jesus Christ."

God's redemptive goal for us includes growing us to know Him. Jesus understood God's goal, and lived on mission pressing on towards that goal. Jesus said in Mark 12:30-31, that we are to love the Lord our God with all heart, with all our soul, with all our mind, and all of our strength. This command is to love God with our entire *being, doing, and knowing*. God understands that there are disordered desires (vices/sin) that will pull us out of the trajectory of oneness with Him. He understands that the practice of virtues in your everyday living is going to be difficult because it will be counter cultural to the way the majority of the world is living. Jesus knew we needed to be one with Him to help us effectively live into God's mission and everything He has for us in that trajectory.

The voice of Paul in Scripture understood the pursuit of living into the trajectory of one-ness with Christ. The following passage is from Philippians, written by Paul. As you read the following epistle, imagine as though Paul has written this letter with you in mind to encourage and exhort you. It seems Paul's heart in ministry is to help people understand the power of doing life with Christ. Paul's passion is to see people pursue living a whole-hearted committed life to Christ and His redeeming second order story. As you read the following passage from Philippians 3:3-21, consider the exhortation and invitation Paul is offering for the trajectory of your life.

"To Know Him Personally"
(Written by Paul in his letter to the Philippians)

Philippians 3:3-21 MSG

3 And that's about it, friends. Be glad in God!

I don't mind repeating what I have written in earlier letters, and I hope you don't mind hearing it again. Better safe than sorry—so here goes.

2-6 Steer clear of the barking dogs, those religious busybodies, all bark and no bite. All they're interested in is appearances—knife-happy circumcisers, I call them. The *real* believers are the ones the Spirit of God leads to work away at this ministry, filling the air with Christ's praise as we do it. We couldn't carry this off by our own efforts, and we know it—even though we can list what many might think are impressive credentials. You know my pedigree: a legitimate birth, circumcised on the eighth day; an Israelite from the elite tribe of Benjamin; a strict and devout adherent to God's law; a fiery defender of the purity of my religion, even to the point of persecuting the church; a meticulous observer of everything set down in God's law Book.

7-9 The very credentials these people are waving around as something special, I'm tearing up and throwing out with the trash—along with everything else I used to take credit for. And why? Because of Christ. Yes, all the things I once thought were so important are gone from my life. Compared to the high privilege of knowing Christ Jesus as my Master, first-hand, everything I once thought I had going for me is insignificant—dog dung. I've dumped it all in the trash so that I could embrace Christ and be embraced by him. I didn't want some petty, inferior brand of righteousness that comes from keeping a list of rules when I could get the robust kind that comes from trusting Christ—*God's* righteousness.

[10-11] I gave up all that inferior stuff so I could know Christ personally, experience his resurrection power, be a partner in his suffering, and go all the way with him to death itself. If there was any way to get in on the resurrection from the dead, I wanted to do it.

Philippians 3:3-21 MSG Continued – Focused on the Goal

[12-14] I'm not saying that I have this all together, that I have it made. But I am well on my way, reaching out for Christ, who has so wondrously reached out for me. Friends, don't get me wrong: By no means do I count myself an expert in all of this, but I've got my eye on the goal, where God is beckoning us onward—to Jesus. I'm off and running, and I'm not turning back.

[15-16] So let's keep focused on that goal, those of us who want everything God has for us. If any of you have something else in mind, something less than total commitment, God will clear your blurred vision—you'll see it yet! Now that we're on the right track, let's stay on it.

[17-19] Stick with me, friends. Keep track of those you see running this same course, headed for this same goal. There

are many out there taking other paths, choosing other goals, and trying to get you to go along with them. I've warned you of them many times; sadly, I'm having to do it again. All they want is easy street. They hate Christ's Cross. But easy street is a dead-end street. Those who live there make their bellies their gods; belches are their praise; all they can think of is their appetites.

[20-21] But there's far more to life for us. We're citizens of high heaven! We're waiting the arrival of the Savior, the Master, Jesus Christ, who will transform our earthly bodies into glorious bodies like his own. He'll make us beautiful and whole with the same powerful skill by which he is putting everything as it should be, under and around him.[29]

This passage of Paul speaking into the language of trajectory and telos, highlighting two different life narratives at work, illuminates Paul's awareness of goals and pathways and how the atmosphere we are plugged into can affect our life trajectory and our becoming in Christ.

- What stood out to you in this passage? Are you inspired? If so, how? What challenged you? What do you need from God?

Day 17, The Cool Down: The Virtue Model

Take a moment to reflect and exhale. Stretch out your thoughts and share with God in prayer. Reflecting on the virtue model, consider as you are and how you are living. In light of God's heart for you and oneness with Him, consider as you could be as you pursue the trajectory of living into His goal for your life. Jesus prayed for you in John 17 right before He was arrested. His longing was for you to know Him personally. To be one with His Father like He was, reconciled, and able to and wanting to do the things that pleased God.

Share with God what is stirring in your heart. What are you wrestling with? What are you encouraged by? Breathe out these thoughts with the Lord, and ask Him to help you live into His story in your own unique story.

Day 18 | The Training Ground: Focusing the Lens

When things are hard and disruptive in life, it is helpful to reframe how we see and think about our circumstances. In psychology, reframing[30] is a powerful skill that can help people shift their thinking about a situation. How we look at our circumstances can help us make the most of a given situation or not. The task at hand is in attempting to reframe and "focus the lens" on what we are chasing, who we are chasing, and to call to mind thinking about how we can make the most of our days now, that will be fruitful in the future.

In partnering with God to work out our salvation, the primary theological dimensions of the virtuous model includes pursuing virtuous pathways and embracing God's overarching narrative that will help lead us towards His teleological goal in life.[31] We have more freedom when we live within the guidelines God offers us than when we live without any guidelines. This is because healthy boundaries provide more freedom to operate safely within, as opposed to less without.[32] For example, consider driving in a car at pace on a bridge over a deep ravine. The barriers on each side of the road help to create a guide and a boundary to move at pace to get you where you are going. Now imagine if the road had no barriers and it was a literal free fall if you slipped a tire off the road. I would likely drive a lot slower and more scared on a border-less bridge versus a walled bridge. God's design of boundaries and morals that are virtuous serve us like that guardrail on the bridge. It creates guidance and protection so that we can move freely and confidently over the ravines in life.

God has created us to desire, which is a good thing. Being able to identify what is a healthy desire and an unhealthy desire mat-ters as we discern the choices we can make. Virtues are ordered desires that nourish and honor life. Virtues include: compassion, tem-perance (patience), magnanimity (generosity), courage, justice, faith, hope, and love. Vices are simply disordered desires that cause disruption to wholeness and satisfaction in our lives. An example of vices include the seven deadly sins: wrath, avarice (greed), slothfulness (laziness), pride, lust, envy, and gluttony. As we learn what virtues are and what vices are, this helps us to know how our choices contribute to our every-day living and the trajectory that they cultivate.

- Reflecting on the adjacent illustration of the Virtue Model, the arrow is now blank. Write down any virtues and practices that are helping you live into and towards God's telos and your *becoming* in Him. Write down any vices, or disorder desires that pull you out of the trajectory of living into God's redemptive goal.

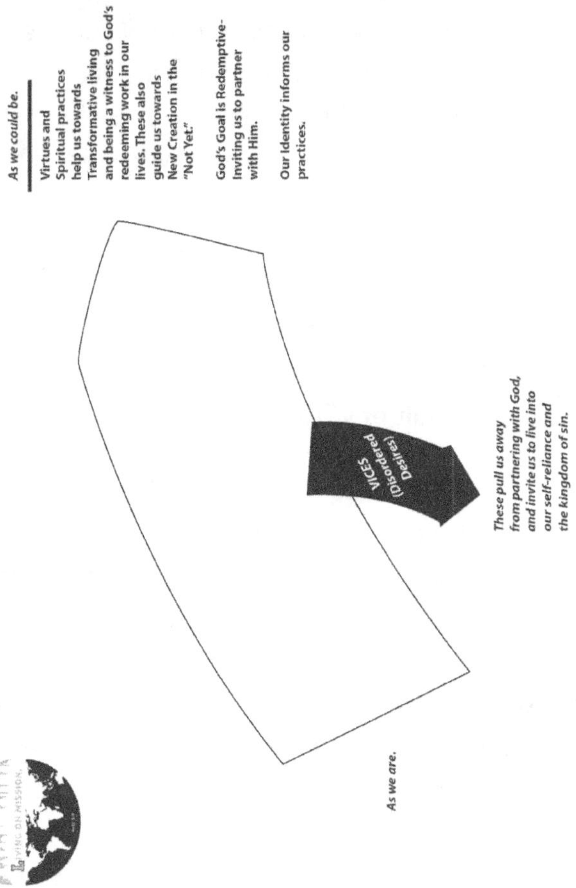

As we could be.

Virtues and Spiritual practices help us towards Transformative living and being a witness to God's redeeming work in our lives. These also guide us towards New Creation in the "Not Yet."

God's Goal is Redemptive- Inviting us to partner with Him.

Our Identity informs our practices.

VICES (Disordered Desires)

These pull us away from partnering with God, and invite us to live into our self-reliance and the kingdom of sin.

As we are.

LIVING ON MISSION

* *This diagram was taught to me through Dr. Lee Camp in Christian Ethics Graduate Course at Lipscomb University*

- What virtues do you find hardest to exercise and practice?
- Are there any vices you know you are practicing, but are finding it difficult to surrender them to the Lord? Be honest with yourself. Be honest with God. He sees you just as you are and desires for you to know Him and trust Him more deeply.
- In reflection of your life's timeline, are there any milestones that came about as a result of virtues, or vices?

It's important to identify the virtues and the vices that we are *doing* and to be honest with ourselves in how we are living. God already understands the why behind our *doing* and *being*. We embrace our true self when we are genuinely honest about how we are choosing to live in our lives. It benefits us to recognize which second order story is most affecting the trajectory of our life. Virtues help us live into the Kingdom of God and His goal for us. Vices draw us deeper into the kingdom of sin, and pull us away from oneness with God. Paul reflected on this in Philippians 3 that we read earlier in this chapter. When we have eyes to see as we could become, and we are authentic to owning as we were, we then can embrace as we are and partner with God in His transformative work in us. Remember that God is working in us so that we will want to do and be able to do the things that please Him.

In Acts 1:8 we read, "But you will receive power when the Holy Spirit comes on you; and you will be my witnesses in Jerusalem, and in all Judea and Samaria, and to the ends of the earth."[33] Theologically and tangibly, the heart of spiritual formation is to invite people into *knowing* Jesus and making Jesus known. As people grow in faith and discover their *being* rooted in the identity of Christ and God's overarching redemptive narrative, people can begin to think eschatologically within their personal lives. The desire for me in athletics spiritual formation is to help athletes and coaches recognize that it is through the power of the Holy Spirit that their lives are empowered, and through the witness of our being, knowing, and doing, we can be a vessel for God to operate in and through to make Jesus known to the ends of the earth. God is on a mission, and within spiritual formation, and in every facet of our lives, we are invited to partner with God and live on mission with Him as witnesses to His overarching redemptive narrative. We are to be a signpost to Jesus through virtuous living, encouraging others to live into God's telos in their own lives as well.

- How does this make you feel? How does this focus the lens on how you can illuminate for others God's goodness and His goal through your personal life?

Day 18, The Cool Down: Focusing the Lens

Spend a few moments reflecting and stretching out your thoughts with God. Tell Him what is stirring in you. Invite Him to listen, and then take a moment and listen to Him. Imagine sitting with Jesus, what might He want to say to you?

The Lord desires to help us discover our true selves and grow us to be more in touch with our knowing, and being, and then see how this shapes and informs our doing. In education, we are on a pathway to achieve a degree that aids us in learning and equipping us for future endeavors. In sport and work, we are on a pathway to develop and mature in our craft, perhaps endeavoring for the next highest level, or prize. To get there, we understand that there is a process to get to where we want to go. Understanding who we are and where we are invited to go helps us embrace the striving, the suffering, and the perseverance necessary to live lives that bring glory to God.

- Where do you want to go in life?
- What do you desire from your life for others?
- What do you think God desires for your life?
- How do the temptation of vices in the immediate sacrifice your future and the goals you desire to accomplish?
- How can living in the Kingdom of God influence your everyday living?

Breathe these answers out to God. Let Him process with you. This is a courageous and virtuous practice. Close in prayer as you feel led. Ask God for what you need. Share with God what you desire. As you feel led, invite Him into helping you live into a virtuous life.

Conclusion

"Our challenge is to unmask the Divine in the natural and name the presence of God in our lives. Created from love, of love and for love, our existence makes no sense apart from Divine love. If God loves and accepts you as a sinner, how can you do less? Self-acceptance always precedes genuine self-surrender and self-transformation. We believe we know how to take care of our needs better than God. We all tend to fashion a god who fits our falsity. We do not find our true self by seeking it. Rather, we find it by seeking God. Jesus is the True Self who shows us by his life how to find our self in relation to God. Our happiness is important to God. That will mean the death of our carefully cultivated false self. This hurts, to say the very least. If I were sinless, the perfect image of God, I could know the God of love. But knowing myself as the sinner enables me to know something more: a God of mercy—something greater, for love responds to what is good and lovable; mercy responds to what is not good and makes it good and lovable, the gift of being myself."

– David Brenner,
The Gift of Being Yourself:
The Sacred Call to Self Discovery

This quote highlights the Gospel need we all have in our personal spiritual formation journey. To seek to unmask and know the Divine, to become more self aware, and receive the Lord's mercy is a sacred gift to self discovery. It takes courage to pay attention to the undercurrent of where we find our worth and become aware of the virtues and vices that we live out in our everyday lives. With this, it is important to focus the lens on what we are pursuing, doing, and becoming. I have discovered that living into the trajectory of His greater story is a pathway to so much more in life! What a gift it is to be ourselves illuminated by Christ.

Thank you for taking the time to walk through this study. My heart and hope is that it helped to be a catalyst and illuminate for you that your worth is way more significant in Christ and His story. Your life matters. Your story matters. Walking from "death to life, life-out-of-death" in Christ matters. Transformation is significant to our spiritual journey, and necessary to grow in Christlikeness. Your gifts, passions, and personality are intended to be an unique expression of Jesus Christ in and through you and your vocation for the blessing and expanding of God's Kingdom. You are the only version of you this world has, and you are needed for such a time as this.

You may be asking, where do I go from here?

1. *Continue to pursue growing in knowing God.* Remember "knowing" as Jesus

prayed in John 17 means to embrace and seek face to face connection with God through prayer. From a spiritual sense, this means to ask God to give you sight to see Him in your everyday living; and to also receive His loving gaze towards you. Just like the blind man in Mark that we read about, Jesus wants to take your hand and be one on one with you away from the crowds. Let Him help you see. As you seek to connect with Jesus, pray and speak to Him as though He were actually sitting with you and attentively listening. Allow Him space to connect with you and your being.

2. *Pursue virtuous living.* Adopt high moral standards for your life. Not in a legalistic way. In a way where there is a thoughtful choice to pursue godliness, and live into reverence towards God in how you are living. Remember that sin causes separation in oneness with God and other people. We can't help being

sinners, but we can help sinning less intentionally. Practice whole-hearted confession and ask God to help you want to and be able to do the things that please Him. Remember He desires oneness with you, just as Jesus asked for on your behalf in John 17. Living into virtues will bless you. It won't always be easy, especially at first when you begin a new habit of living. Just like exercise, flexing new muscles can be uncomfortable, and yet, become incredibly rewarding as it strengthens you and your life. Especially, when you seek to get the most out of the workout.

3. *Pursue becoming.* Today, we are just as we are, and likely, there are aspirations and desires to become as you could be. Pursue the trajectory that guides you towards God's goal – to live into His redemptive narrative that offers your story incredible value and opportunity to be empowered by His Greater Story.

Your worth, identity and significance has eternal value to Christ. Pursue becoming content and at peace with being His beloved. You are a living letter, allow Him to illuminate your story with His goodness. Ask God to help you live into your life empowered by His Holy Spirit.

To do these things, I encourage you to find faith companions that will help you grow in this trajectory. Christ centered Spiritual Direction and healthy Christ centered counseling are wonderful resources. As are community groups, and solid brothers and sisters in Christ who are also running towards God and knowing Him more deeply. Trustworthy faith companions are a gift to help you live into God's goal on this side of Heaven. If you are having trouble identifying who those people could be in your life, ask God to provide them. Ask God to help you connect and be united with people who will help you grow in knowing Christ, and making Christ known. If desired, a few resources are available at the end of this book.

Remember, our calling is to live into the mission of God, while fellowshipping with the Trinity and other people. Jesus wants us to grow in knowing Him more and more which in turn helps us grow in knowing ourselves made in and through Him. Our worth is to be found in Christ and what He has done, is doing, and will be doing. This is hard for us to comprehend in the initial discovery of realizing that there are two stories at play, one of the world and one of Christ and His Kingdom. As hard as it can be to shift our thinking, we are asked to do so in Scripture. We are told to take our thoughts captive before the knowledge of Christ and intentionally seek to renew our minds in and through His Holy Spirit. You are a chosen Ambassador for Christ and He desires to activate your life more and more in and through Him for the sake of this world. You are Divinely approved. You are made righteous through Christ, and are part of the functional and aesthetic design of redemption. Your personal story has the opportunity to be deepened and illuminated as a credible commentary to God's story. The trajectory of your life and living into a pathway to more life in Christ has eternal value. I hope you are encouraged to go and make the most of your days. After all, the Kingdom of God and this world is blessed as a result of us all doing so.

Blessings and gratitude as you grow in knowing Whose you are and who you are in Him. You matter and are significant to God and His story in the tension of the now and the not yet.

Acknowledgment

For those that have walked with me and disci-pled me, prayed for me, and extended grace truth, and mercy to me, thank you. As I have writ-ten this, my heart has been to share with others what I have grown in learning and trusting. What I have written, I share in reverence for God's truth and from the best as I have understood so far. I pray for what is true to be life giving to those that read this book. Lord Jesus, thank you for loving us just as we are, and beckoning us to pursue and follow after you. I am grateful Lord that Your life and purpose offers us life and pur-pose. Be with these readers, and may they grow in knowing you more deeply throughout all of their days.

Thank you to my children and husband, and extended family, who have supported me while studying, writing, and coaching. I am grateful for your love, grace, and truth.

Thank you to MAI, AIA, FCA, Belle's Bible Study, and Meck church for being a sign post to Jesus and providing community to be known, and make Jesus known.

Thank you, Lipscomb, and to all my professors there who helped guide me and others to growing in knowing Jesus more. Thank you for asking hard questions and beckoning me to more life in Christ.

Thank you, Sherri, Tiffany, and Karen, for serving me in Spiritual Direction and inviting me to sit and embrace the face of Jesus.

Thank you to every teammate, student-athlete and student I have had the privilege to walk with at some point in my life. You matter to Jesus, and your life has impacted me, thank you for being you.

I am eternally grateful.

References

[1] Caine, Christine. (2016) Unashamed Study. Run, Don't Hide. Video 1. Zondervan: Retrieved from https://www.youtube.com/watch?v=ZXIctTLaCF4

[2] Strongs Concordance: Blue Letter Bible Greek and Hebrew Lexicon. https://www.blueletterbible.org/lang/lexicon/lexicon.cfm?Strongs=G1343&t=CSB

[3] Strongs Concordance: Blue Letter Bible Greek and Hebrew Lexicon. https://www.blueletterbible.org/lang/lexicon/lexicon.cfm?Strongs=G3742&t=NIV

[4] Strongs Concordance & Lexicon: Blue Letter Bible. https://www.blueletterbible.org/lang/lexicon/lexicon.cfm?Strongs=H7068&t=CSB

5   Strongs Concordance, www.biblehub.com/greek/1495.html

6   Strongs Concordance 2889. Kosmos. Retrieved from: https://biblehub.com/greek/2889.htm

7   Strongs Concordance: Blue Letter Bible. https://www.blueletterbible.org/lang/lexicon/lexicon.cfm?Strongs=G1401&t=CSB

8   Caine, C. 2016. Run, Don't Hide Video. Unashamed Study.

9   Strongs Concordance. (1987) Helps Ministry, Bible Hub. http://biblehub.com/greek/4053.htm

10   Lavender, Earl. (2018) Missional Strategies Lecture. Unit 3A: Mission in Culture. Tegrity Course Lecture.

11   Strongs Concordance. Bible Hub: Repent, 3340. http://biblehub.com/greek/3340.htm

[12] Philippians 2:13 1993. Philippians 2:13 CEB. Retrieved from: https://www.biblegateway.com/passage/?search=Philippians%20 2:12-14&version=CEB

[13] Gorman, Michael J. 2015. Becoming the Gospel: Paul, Participation, and Mission. Michigan: Wm. B. Eerdmans Publishing Co. p. 197-199)

[14] **Amplified Bible** (AMP) (2015) Bible Gateway. Amplified Bible Translation. Philippians 2:12-13. https://www. biblegateway.com/passage/?search=Philippians+2:12-14&version=AMP. The Lockman Foundation, La Habra, CA.

[15] **Amplified Bible** (AMP) (2015) Bible Gateway. Amplified Bible Translation. Philippians 2:12-13. https://www. biblegateway.com/passage/?search=Philippians+2:12-14&version=AMP. The Lockman Foundation, La Habra, CA.

16   Gorman, Michael J. 2015. Becoming the
      Gospel: Paul, Participation, and Mission.
      Michigan: Wm. B. Eerdmans Publishing Co.
      Becoming and Telling the Story of Christ:
      Philippians, 108-113.

17   NIV Study Bible. (1983) Commentary Notes
      on Ezekiel 36:24-27. p.1297

18   Ruis, David. 2005. Vineyard Voices: The
      Worship Series, Every Move I Make.
      Vineyard Worship. Song: Lilly of the Valley.

19   Caine, Christine. 2016. Unashamed:
      Run, Don't Hide. Video 1. Zondervan:
      Retrieved from https://www.youtube.com/
      watch?v=ZXIctTLaCF4

20   Root, Andrew. 2014. Christopraxis:
      A Practical Theology of the Cross.
      Minneapolis: Fortress Press. Dominant
      Models of Practical Theology, 81.

[21] Amplified Bible (AMP). (2015) The Lockman Foundation. Jeremiah 29:11-13. https://www.biblegateway.com/passage/?search=-Jeremiah+29%3A11-13&version=AMP

[22] Strongs Concordance. (1998) NAS Exhaustive Concordance of the Bible with Hebrew-Aramaic and Greek Dictionaries. Bible Hub. http://biblehub.com/hebrew/7965.html

[23] Frankl, Viktor. 2006. *Man's Search for Meaning*. Boston, MA: Beacon Press. Part II: Logotherapy, The Meaning of Life, 108.

[24] White, James Emery. Mecklenburg Community Church Message. Charlotte, NC. 2011

[25] Meck Institute Spiritual Gifts Assessment: https://mecker.typeform.com/to/c11y32ys

Churchgrowth.org Spiritual Gifts Survey: http://gifts.churchgrowth.org/spiritual-gifts-survey/

Spiritual Gifts Test: https://spiritualgiftstest.com/my-account/

26   Camp, Dr. Lee. Christian Ethics Graduate Course: Class Lecture Notes. Lipscomb University, Fall 2020.

27   Harrison, Nonna Verra. *God's Many Splendored Image: Theological Anthropology for Christian Formation.* Baker Academic. 2010

28   Strongs Concordance, Greek Lexicon for Ginosko. Retrieved from: https://biblehub.com/lexicon/john/17-3.htm

29   Philippians 3:3-21 MSG

30   One of the skills to help us develop as mature, resilient individuals is that of *reframing*. When we change our point of view on any given situation, the facts remain the same, but a deliberate shift is made in how we see it. "Reframing: The Transformative Power of Suffering." Psychology Today. December 14, 2017. Retrieved from: https://www.psychologytoday.com/us/blog/

stronger-the-broken-places/201712/
reframing

31   Wadell, Paul J. *Happiness and the Christian
      Moral Life: An Introduction to Christian
      Ethics.* Rowman & Littlefield Publishers; 3rd
      Edition. 2016.

32   Wadell, Paul J. *Happiness and the Christian
      Moral Life: An Introduction to Christian
      Ethics.* Rowman & Littlefield Publishers; 3rd
      Edition. 2016. (140)

33   The Holy Bible. Acts 1:8, NIV. Zondervan,
      MI.

Resources

– Spiritual Direction –

Sustainable Faith
https://sustainablefaith.com/

Grafted Life Ministries
https://www.graftedlife.org/
spiritual-direction/esda

Holding Hope Together with Sherri Harder
www.holdinghopetogether.com

The Rested Nest with Tiffany Bird
https://www.therestednest.org/

Lipscomb University
Institute of Christian Spirituality
https://www.lipscomb.edu/ics

Your Enneagram Coach
https://www.yourenneagramcoach.com/

Enneagram & Life Coaching with Danielle Smith
https://www.vocarecoaching.com/

– Assessments –

Meck Institute Spiritual Gifts Assessment:
https://mecker.typeform.com/to/c11y32ys

Churchgrowth.org Spiritual Gifts Survey:
https://gifts.churchgrowth.org/spiritual-gifts-survey/

Spiritual Gifts Test:
https://spiritualgiftstest.com/my-account/